Full Color on Every Page!

Windows

— 98 —

VISUAL POCKETGUIDE™

IDG's **3-D Visual** Series

IDG BOOKS *From* **maranGraphics™**

IDG Books Worldwide, Inc.
An International Data Group Company
Foster City, CA • Indianapolis • Chicago • Southlake, TX

ii

Windows® 98 Visual PocketGuide™

Published by
IDG Books Worldwide, Inc.
An International Data Group Company
919 E. Hillsdale Blvd., Suite 400
Foster City, CA 94404
(650) 655-3000

Copyright© 1998 by maranGraphics Inc.
    5755 Coopers Avenue
    Mississauga, Ontario, Canada
    L4Z 1R9

All rights reserved. No part of this book, including interior design, cover design, and icons, may be reproduced or transmitted in any form, by any means (electronic, photocopying, recording, or otherwise) without prior written permission from maranGraphics.

Library of Congress Catalog Card No.: 98-85136
ISBN: 0-7645-6035-2
Printed in the United States of America
10 9 8 7 6 5 4 3 2

Distributed in the United States by IDG Books Worldwide, Inc.

Distributed by Transworld Publishers Limited in the United Kingdom; by IDG Norge Books for Norway; by IDG Sweden Books for Sweden; by Woodslane Pty. Ltd. for Australia; by Woodslane Enterprises Ltd. for New Zealand; by Longman Singapore Publishers Ltd. for Singapore, Malaysia, Thailand, and Indonesia; by Simron Pty. Ltd. for South Africa; by Toppan Company Ltd. for Japan; by Distribuidora Cuspide for Argentina; by Livraria Cultura for Brazil; by Ediciencia S.A. for Ecuador; by Addison-Wesley Publishing Company for Korea; by Ediciones ZETA S.C.R. Ltda. for Peru; by WS Computer Publishing Corporation, Inc., for the Philippines; by Unalis Corporation for Taiwan; by Contemporanea de Ediciones for Venezuela; by Computer Book & Magazine Store for Puerto Rico; by Express Computer Distributors for the Caribbean and West Indies. Authorized Sales Agent: Anthony Rudkin Associates for the Middle East and North Africa.

For corporate orders, please call maranGraphics at 800-469-6616.
For general information on IDG Books Worldwide's books in the U.S., please call our Consumer Customer Service department at 800-762-2974.
For reseller information, including discounts and premium sales, please call our Reseller Customer Service department at 800-434-3422.
For information on where to purchase IDG Books Worldwide's books outside the U.S., please contact our International Sales department at 650-655-3200 or fax 650-655-3295.
For information on foreign language translations, please contact our Foreign & Subsidiary Rights department at 650-655-3021 or fax 650-655-3281.
For sales inquiries and special prices for bulk quantities, please contact our Sales department at 650-655-3200.
For information on using IDG Books Worldwide's books in the classroom or for ordering examination copies, please contact our Educational Sales department at 800-434-2086 or fax 817-251-8174.
For press review copies, author interviews, or other publicity information, please contact our Public Relations department at 650-655-3000 or fax 650-655-3299.
For authorization to photocopy items for corporate, personal, or educational use, please contact maranGraphics at 800-469-6616.

LIMIT OF LIABILITY/DISCLAIMER OF WARRANTY: AUTHOR AND PUBLISHER HAVE USED THEIR BEST EFFORTS IN PREPARING THIS BOOK. IDG BOOKS WORLDWIDE, INC., AND AUTHOR MAKE NO REPRESENTATIONS OR WARRANTIES WITH RESPECT TO THE ACCURACY OR COMPLETENESS OF THE CONTENTS OF THIS BOOK AND SPECIFICALLY DISCLAIM ANY IMPLIED WARRANTIES OF MERCHANTABILITY OR FITNESS FOR A PARTICULAR PURPOSE. THERE ARE NO WARRANTIES WHICH EXTEND BEYOND THE DESCRIPTIONS CONTAINED IN THIS PARAGRAPH. NO WARRANTY MAY BE CREATED OR EXTENDED BY SALES REPRESENTATIVES OR WRITTEN SALES MATERIALS. THE ACCURACY AND COMPLETENESS OF THE INFORMATION PROVIDED HEREIN AND THE OPINIONS STATED HEREIN ARE NOT GUARANTEED OR WARRANTED TO PRODUCE ANY PARTICULAR RESULTS, AND THE ADVICE AND STRATEGIES CONTAINED HEREIN MAY NOT BE SUITABLE FOR EVERY INDIVIDUAL. NEITHER IDG BOOKS WORLDWIDE, INC., NOR AUTHOR SHALL BE LIABLE FOR ANY LOSS OF PROFIT OR ANY OTHER COMMERCIAL DAMAGES, INCLUDING BUT NOT LIMITED TO SPECIAL, INCIDENTAL, CONSEQUENTIAL, OR OTHER DAMAGES. FULFILLMENT OF EACH COUPON OFFER IS THE RESPONSIBILITY OF THE OFFEROR.

Trademark Acknowledgments

maranGraphics Inc. has attempted to include trademark information
for products, services and companies referred to in this guide. Although
maranGraphics Inc. has made reasonable efforts in gathering this
information, it cannot guarantee its accuracy.

All brand names and product names used in this book are trade
names, service marks, trademarks, or registered trademarks of their
respective owners. IDG Books Worldwide and maranGraphics Inc.
are not associated with any product or vendor mentioned in this book.

FOR PURPOSES OF ILLUSTRATING THE CONCEPTS AND TECHNIQUES
DESCRIBED IN THIS BOOK, THE AUTHOR HAS CREATED VARIOUS NAMES,
COMPANY NAMES, MAILING ADDRESSES, E-MAIL ADDRESSES AND PHONE
NUMBERS, ALL OF WHICH ARE FICTITIOUS. ANY RESEMBLANCE OF THESE
FICTITIOUS NAMES, COMPANY NAMES, MAILING ADDRESSES, E-MAIL
ADDRESSES AND PHONE NUMBERS TO ANY ACTUAL PERSON, COMPANY
AND/OR ORGANIZATION IS UNINTENTIONAL AND PURELY COINCIDENTAL.

maranGraphics has used their best efforts in preparing this book.
As Web sites are constantly changing, some of the Web site addresses
in this book may have moved or no longer exist.
maranGraphics does not accept responsibility nor liability for losses
or damages resulting from the information contained in this book.
maranGraphics also does not support the views expressed in the
Web sites contained in this book.
Screen shots displayed in this book are based on pre-release software
and are subject to change.

Permissions

CBS SportsLine
© 1996 SportsLine USA, Inc. http://www.sportsline.com
All rights reserved.

CNN/SI
© 1998 Cable News Network, Inc. All rights reserved.
Used by permission of CNN/SI.

Microsoft Home Page
Screen shots reprinted with permission from Microsoft Corporation.

MSNBC Weather Map
© MSNBC on the Internet, 1998.

The Smithsonian
© 1996 by Smithsonian Institution.

YAHOO!
© 1996 by YAHOO!, Inc. All rights reserved. YAHOO! and the
YAHOO! logo are trademarks of YAHOO!, Inc.

**Permissions have also been granted for the following
screen shots:**
Discovery Channel Online
Florida Legislature - Online Sunshine
Flower Stop
Minolta
People Online - The Daily
Sunkist
Travel Source

U.S. Corporate Sales

Contact maranGraphics
at (800) 469-6616
or fax (905) 890-9434.

U.S. Trade Sales

Contact IDG Books
at (800) 434-3422
or (650) 655-3000.

© 1998 maranGraphics, Inc.
The animated characters are the
copyright of maranGraphics, Inc.

Welcome to the world of IDG Books Worldwide.

IDG Books Worldwide, Inc., is a subsidiary of International Data Group, the world's largest publisher of computer-related information and the leading global provider of information services on information technology. IDG was founded more than 25 years ago and now employs more than 8,500 people worldwide. IDG publishes more than 270 computer publications in over 75 countries (see listing below). More than 90 million people read one or more IDG publications each month.

Launched in 1990, IDG Books Worldwide is today the #1 publisher of best-selling computer books in the United States. We are proud to have received eight awards from the Computer Press Association in recognition of editorial excellence and three from Computer Currents' First Annual Readers' Choice Awards. Our best-selling ...For Dummies® series has more than 25 million copies in print with translations in 30 languages. IDG Books Worldwide, through a joint venture with IDG's Hi-Tech Beijing, became the first U.S. publisher to publish a computer book in the People's Republic of China. In record time, IDG Books Worldwide has become the first choice for millions of readers around the world who want to learn how to better manage their businesses.

Our mission is simple: Every one of our books is designed to bring extra value and skill-building instructions to the reader. Our books are written by experts who understand and care about our readers. The knowledge base of our editorial staff comes from years of experience in publishing, education, and journalism - experience which we use to produce books for the '90s. In short, we care about books, so we attract the best people. We devote special attention to details such as audience, interior design, use of icons, and illustrations. And because we use an efficient process of authoring, editing, and desktop publishing our books electronically, we can spend more time ensuring superior content and spend less time on the technicalities of making books.

You can count on our commitment to deliver high-quality books at competitive prices on topics you want to read about. At IDG Books Worldwide, we continue in the IDG tradition of delivering quality for more than 25 years. You'll find no better book on a subject than one from IDG Books Worldwide.

John Kilcullen
President and CEO
IDG Books Worldwide, Inc.

IDG Books Worldwide, Inc., is a subsidiary of International Data Group, the world's largest publisher of computer-related information and the leading global provider of information services on information technology. International Data Group publishes over 276 computer publications in over 75 countries. Ninety million people read one or more International Data Group publications each month. International Data Group's publications include: Argentina: Annuario de Informatica, Computerworld Argentina, PC World Argentina; Australia: Australian Macworld, Client/Server Journal, Computer Living, Computerworld, Computerworld 100, Digital News, IT Casebook, Network World, On-line World Australia, PC World, Publishing Essentials, Reseller, WebMaster; Austria: Computerwelt Osterreich, Networks Austria, PC Tip; Belarus: PC World Belarus; Belgium: Data News; Brazil: Annuário de Informática, Computerworld Brazil, Connections, Super Game Power, Macworld, PC Player, PC World Brazil, Publish Brazil, Reseller News; Bulgaria: Computerworld Bulgaria, Networkworld/Bulgaria, PC & MacWorld Bulgaria; Canada: CIO Canada, Client/Server World, ComputerWorld Canada, InfoCanada, Network World Canada; Chile: Computerworld Chile, PC World Chile; Colombia: Computerworld Colombia, PC World Colombia; Costa Rica: PC World Centro America; The Czech and Slovak Republics: Computerworld Czechoslovakia, Elektronika Czechoslovakia, Macworld Czech Republic, PC World Czechoslovakia; Denmark: Communications World, Computerworld Danmark, Macworld Danmark, PC Privat Danmark, PC World Danmark, PC World Danmark Supplements, TECH World; Dominican Republic: PC World Republica Dominicana; Ecuador: PC World Ecuador; Egypt: Computerworld Middle East, PC World Middle East; El Salvador: PC World Centro America; Finland: MikroPC, Tietoverkko, Tietoviikko; France: Distributique, Golden, Hebdo-Distributique, Info PC, Le Guide du Monde Informatique, Le Monde Informatique, Reseaux & Telecoms; Germany: Computer Partner, Computerwoche, Computerwoche Extra, Computerwoche Focus, I/M Information Management, Macwelt, PC Welt; Greece: GamePro, Multimedia World; Guatemala: PC World Centro America; Honduras: PC World Centro America; Hong Kong: Computerworld Hong Kong, PCWorld Hong Kong, Publish in Asia; Hungary: ABCD CD-ROM, Computerworld Szamitastechnika, PC & Mac World Hungary, PC-X Magazine; Iceland: Tolvuheimur/PC World Island; India: Information Systems Computerworld, PC World India, Publish in Asia; Indonesia: InfoKomputer PC World, Komputek Computerworld, Publish in Asia; Ireland: ComputerScope, PC Live!; Israel: People & Computers; Italy: Computerworld Italia, Computerworld Italia Special Editions, Macworld Italia, Networking Italia, PC Shopping, PC World Italia, PC World/Walt Disney; Japan: DTP World, HP Open World Japan, Macworld Japan, Nikkei Personal Computing, Open World Japan, OS/2 World Japan, SunWorld Japan, Windows World Japan; Kenya: East African Computer News; Korea: Hi-Tech Information/Computerworld, Macworld Korea, PC World Korea; Macedonia: PC World Macedonia; Malaysia: Computerworld Malaysia, PC World Malaysia, Publish in Asia; Mexico: Computerworld Mexico, Macworld, PC World Mexico; Myanmar: PC World Myanmar; Netherlands: Computer! Totaal, LAN Magazine, LanWorld Buyers Guide, Macworld, Net Magazine, Totaal! Beurskrant; New Zealand: Absolute Beginner's Guide, Computer Buyer, Computer Industry Directory, Computerworld New Zealand, MTB, Network World, PC World New Zealand; Nicaragua: PC World Centro America; Nigeria: PC World Nigeria; Norway: Computerworld Norge, Computerworld Privat (Datamagasinet), CW Rapport Norge, IDG's KURSGUIDE, Macworld Norge, Multimediaworld, PC World Ekspress, PC World Nettverk, PC World Norge, PC World's Produktguide, Windows World Spesial; Pakistan: Computerworld Pakistan, PC World Pakistan; Panama: PC World Panama; P. R. of China: China Computer Users, China Computerworld, China Infoworld, China Telecom World Weekly, Computer & Communication, Electronic Design China, Electronics Today, Electronics Weekly, Game Camp, Game Soft, Network World China, PC World China, Popular Computer Weekly, Software Weekly, Software World, Telecom World; Peru: Computerworld Peru, PC World Profesional Peru, PC World Peru; Poland: Computerworld Poland, Computerworld Special Report, Macworld, Networld, PC World Komputer; Philippines: Computerworld Philippines, PC World Philippines, Publish in Asia; Portugal: Cerebro/PC World, Computerworld/Correio Informático, Dealer World Portugal, Mac*In/PC*In, Multimedia World Portugal; Puerto Rico: PC World Puerto Rico; Romania: Computerworld Romania, PC World Romania, Telecom Romania; Russia: Computerworld Russia, Mir PK, Sety; Singapore: Computerworld Singapore, PC World Singapore, Publish in Asia; Slovenia: MONITOR; South Africa: Computing S.A., InfoWorld S.A., Network World S.A., Software World; Spain: Computerworld Espa-a, COMUNICACIONES WORLD, Dealer World, Macworld Espa-a, PC World Espa-a; Sweden: CAP&Design, Computer Sweden, Corporate Computing, MacWorld, Maxi Data, MikroDatorn, Nätverk & Kommunikation, PC/Aktiv, PC World, Windows World; Switzerland: Computerworld Schweiz, Macworld Schweiz, PCtip; Taiwan: Computerworld Taiwan, Macworld Taiwan, PC World Taiwan, Publish Taiwan, Windows World; Thailand: Thai Computerworld, Publish in Asia; Turkey: Computerworld Turkiye, MACWORLD Turkiye, PC WORLD Turkiye; Ukraine: Computerworld Kiev, Computers & Software, Multimedia World Ukraine, PC World Ukraine; United Kingdom: Acorn User, Amiga Action, Amiga Computing, Appletalk, Computing, GamePro, Macworld, Network News, Parents and Computers, PC Advisor, PC Home, PSX Pro UK, The WEB; United States: Cable in the Classroom, CD Review, CIO Magazine, Computerworld, Computerworld Client/Server Journal, Digital Video Magazine, DOS World, Federal Computer Week, GamePro, InfoWorld, I-Way, JavaWorld, Macworld, Multimedia World, Netscape World Online, Network World, PC Entertainment, PC World, Publish, SunWorld Online, SWATPro Magazine, Video Event, WebMaster; Uruguay: PC World Uruguay; Venezuela: Computerworld Venezuela, PC World Venezuela; and Vietnam: PC World Vietnam.

v

Every maranGraphics book represents the extraordinary vision and commitment of a unique family: the Maran family of Toronto, Canada.

Back Row (from left to right):
Sherry Maran, Rob Maran,
Richard Maran, Maxine Maran, Jill Maran.
Front Row (from left to right):
Judy Maran, Ruth Maran.

Richard Maran is the company founder and its inspirational leader. He developed maranGraphics' proprietary communication technology called "visual grammar." This book is built on that technology—empowering readers with the easiest and quickest way to learn about computers.

Ruth Maran is the Author and Architect—a role Richard established that now bears Ruth's distinctive touch. She creates the words and visual structure that are the basis for the books.

Judy Maran is the Project Manager. She works with Ruth, Richard, and the highly talented maranGraphics illustrators, designers, and editors to transform Ruth's material into its final form.

Rob Maran is the Technical and Production Specialist. He makes sure the state-of-the-art technology used to create these books always performs as it should.

Jill Maran is a jack-of-all-trades who works in the Accounting and Human Resources department.

Maxine Maran is the Business Manager and family sage. She maintains order in the business and family—and keeps everything running smoothly.

Credits

Author & Architect: Ruth Maran	**Editors:** Janice Boyer, Vicki Harford, Frances LoPresti, Raquel Scott	**Illustrators:** Russ Marini, Treena Lees, Peter Grecco
Copy Editors: Jill Maran, Kelleigh Wing	**Layout Designer & Illustrator:** Jamie Bell	**Indexer:** Raquel Scott
Project Manager: Judy Maran	**Screens & Illustrations:** Jeff Jones	**Post Production:** Robert Maran
		Editorial Support: Michael Roney

Acknowledgments

Thanks to the dedicated staff of maranGraphics, including Jamie Bell, Cathy Benn, Janice Boyer, Jason M. Brown, Francisco Ferreira, Peter Grecco, Vicki Harford, Jeff Jones, Michelle Kirchner, Wanda Lawrie, Treena Lees, Frances LoPresti, Michael W. McDonald, Jill Maran, Judy Maran, Maxine Maran, Robert Maran, Sherry Maran, Russ Marini, James Menzies, Raquel Scott, Roxanne Van Damme, Paul Whitehead and Kelleigh Wing.

Finally, to Richard Maran who originated the easy-to-use graphic format of this guide. Thank you for your inspiration and guidance.

TABLE OF CONTENTS

WINDOWS BASICS

CREATE DOCUMENTS

TABLE OF CONTENTS

CUSTOMIZE WINDOWS

OPTIMIZE YOUR COMPUTER

PARTS OF THE WINDOWS 98 SCREEN

The Windows 98 screen displays various items. The items that appear depend on how your computer is set up.

My Computer

Lets you view all the folders and files stored on your computer.

Taskbar

Displays a button for each open window on your screen. You can use these buttons to switch between the open windows.

My Documents

Provides a convenient place to store your documents.

Channel Bar

Displays special Web sites that Windows can automatically deliver to your computer.

Internet Explorer

Lets you access Internet Explorer so you can browse the Web.

Desktop

The background area of your screen.

Network Neighborhood

Lets you view all the folders and files available on your network.

Window

A rectangle on your screen that displays information.

Recycle Bin

Stores deleted files and allows you to recover them later.

Title Bar

Displays the name of an open window.

Start Button

Gives you quick access to programs, files and Windows Help.

USING THE MOUSE

A mouse is a handheld device that lets you select and move items on your screen.

MOUSE ACTIONS

Click

Press and release the left mouse button.

Double-click

Quickly press and release the left mouse button twice.

When you move the mouse on your desk, the mouse pointer on your screen moves in the same direction. The mouse pointer assumes different shapes, such as ⌖ or I , depending on its location on your screen and the task you are performing.

Resting your hand on the mouse, use your thumb and two rightmost fingers to move the mouse on your desk. Use your two remaining fingers to press the mouse buttons.

Right-click

Press and release the right mouse button.

Drag

Position the mouse pointer over an object on your screen and then press and hold down the left mouse button. Still holding down the button, move the mouse to where you want to place the object and then release the button.

START WINDOWS

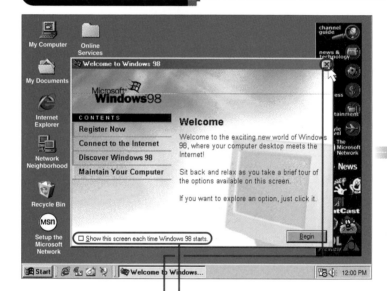

1 Turn on your computer.

■ The Welcome to Windows 98 dialog box appears.

2 If you do not want this dialog box to appear each time you start Windows, move the mouse ☆ over this option and then press the left button (☑ changes to ☐).

3 To close the dialog box, move the mouse ☆ over ☒ and then press the left button.

Windows provides
an easy, graphical way for
you to use your computer.
Windows starts when you
turn on your computer.

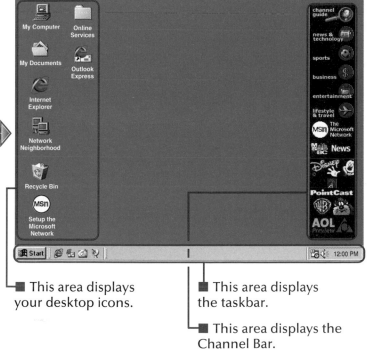

■ This area displays
your desktop icons.

■ This area displays
the taskbar.

■ This area displays the
Channel Bar.

*Note: To remove the Channel Bar,
see page 236.*

START A PROGRAM

START A PROGRAM

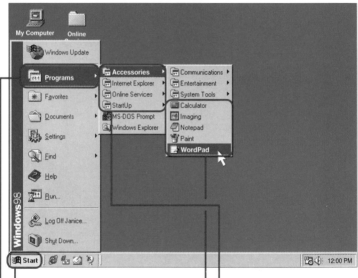

1 To display the Start menu, move the mouse ⌖ over **Start** and then press the left button.

2 To display the programs available on your computer, move the mouse ⌖ over **Programs**.

3 To view additional programs, move the mouse ⌖ over a menu item displaying an arrow (▶).

4 Move the mouse ⌖ over the program you want to start and then press the left button.

You can use the
Start button to start
your programs.

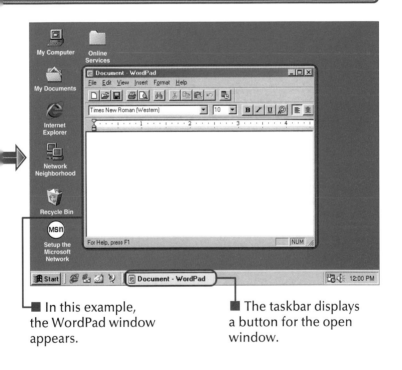

■ In this example,
the WordPad window
appears.

■ The taskbar displays
a button for the open
window.

MAXIMIZE A WINDOW

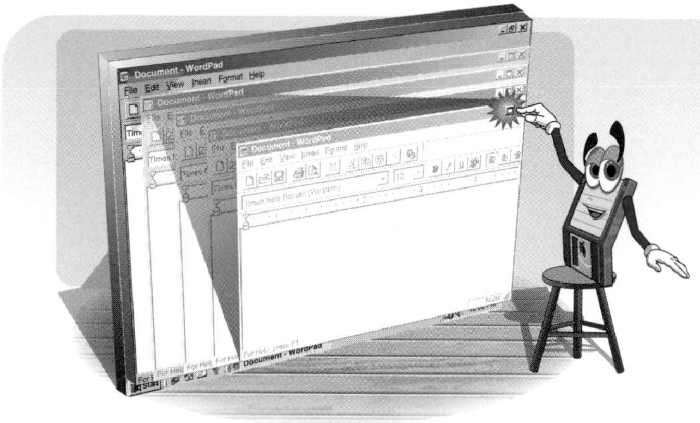

MAXIMIZE A WINDOW

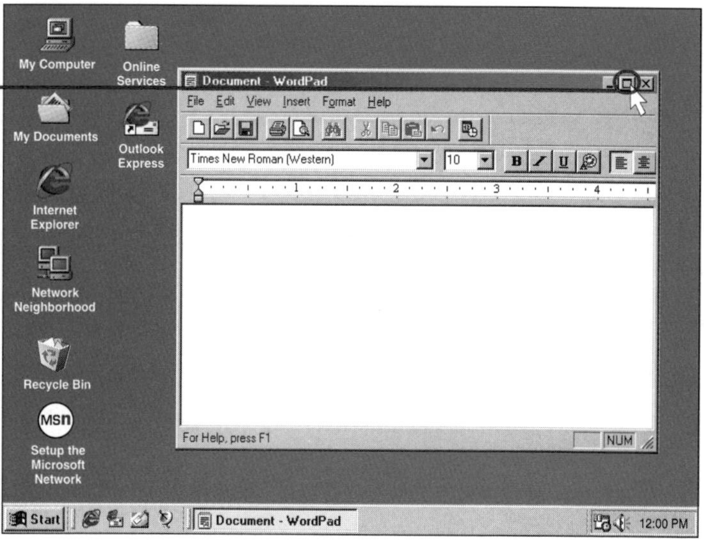

1 Move the mouse over ▢ in the window you want to maximize and then press the left button.

You can enlarge a window to fill your screen. This lets you view more of the window's contents.

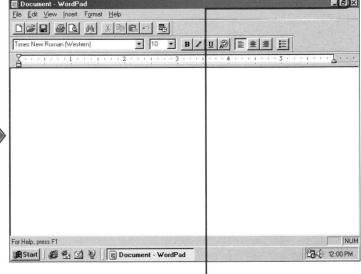

■ The window fills your screen.

■ To return the window to its previous size, move the mouse ⤢ over 🗗 and then press the left button.

11

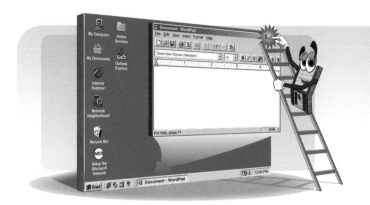

MINIMIZE A WINDOW

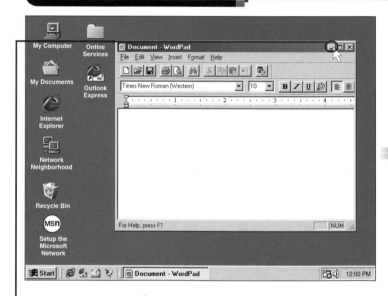

1 Move the mouse ⬚ over ⬚ in the window you want to minimize and then press the left button.

If you are not using a window, you can minimize the window to remove it from your screen. You can redisplay the window at any time.

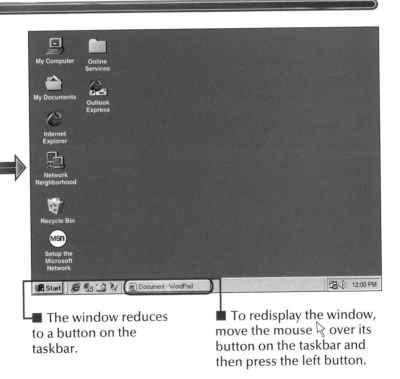

■ The window reduces to a button on the taskbar.

■ To redisplay the window, move the mouse ⌖ over its button on the taskbar and then press the left button.

13

MOVE A WINDOW

MOVE A WINDOW

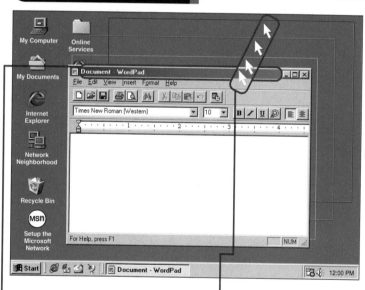

1 Position the mouse ⟍ over the title bar of the window you want to move.

2 Press and hold down the left button as you drag the mouse ⟍ to where you want to place the window.

14

If a window covers items on your screen, you can move the window to a different location.

■ The window moves to the new location.

15

SIZE A WINDOW

SIZE A WINDOW

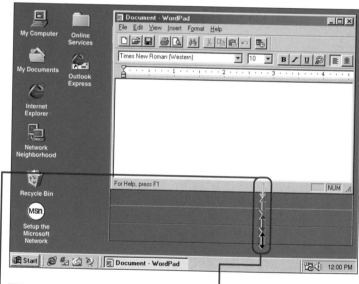

1 Position the mouse ⌐ over an edge of the window you want to size (⌐ changes to ↕, ↔ or ↘).

2 Press and hold down the left button as you drag the mouse ↕ until the window displays the size you want.

You can easily change the size of a window displayed on your screen.

Enlarging a window lets you view more of its contents. Reducing a window lets you view items covered by the window.

■ The window displays the new size.

17

SCROLL THROUGH A WINDOW

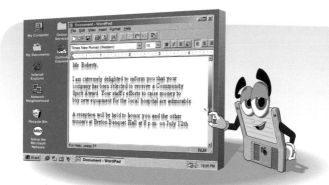

SCROLL UP OR DOWN

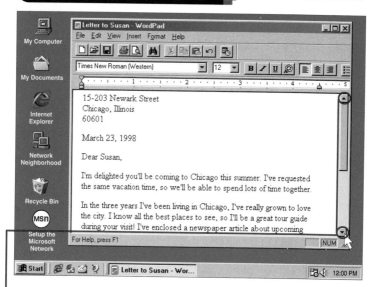

1 To scroll up or down through the information in a window, move the mouse ⤢ over ▲ or ▼ and then press the left button.

You can use a scroll bar to browse through the information in a window. This is useful when a window is not large enough to display all the information it contains.

SCROLL TO ANY POSITION

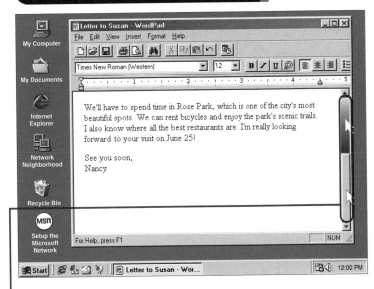

1 Press and hold down the left button as you drag the scroll box along the scroll bar until the information you want to view appears.

■ The location of the scroll box indicates which part of the window you are viewing. For example, when the scroll box is halfway down the scroll bar, you are viewing information from the middle of the window.

19

SWITCH BETWEEN WINDOWS

SWITCH BETWEEN WINDOWS

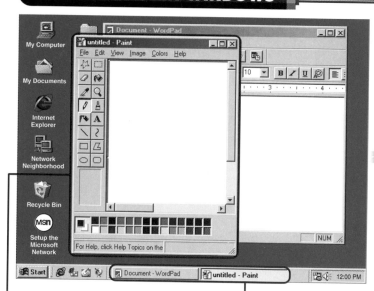

■ You can work in only one window at a time. The active window (example: Paint) appears in front of all other windows and displays a blue title bar.

■ The taskbar displays a button for each open window.

You can have more
than one window open at a
time. You can easily switch
between all the windows
you have open.

Each window is like a separate
piece of paper. Switching between
windows lets you place a different
piece of paper at the top of the pile.

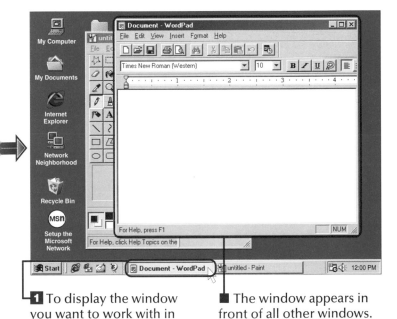

1 To display the window
you want to work with in
front of all other windows,
move the mouse ⬥ over its
button on the taskbar and
then press the left button.

■ The window appears in
front of all other windows.
This lets you clearly view
the contents of the window.

21

CLOSE A WINDOW

CLOSE A WINDOW

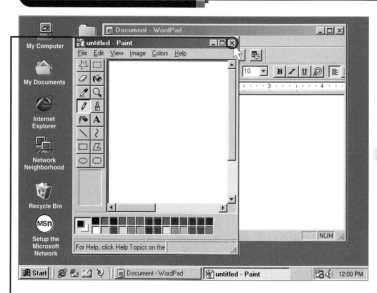

1 Move the mouse ⌖ over ✕ in the window you want to close and then press the left button.

22

When you finish working with a window, you can close the window to remove it from your screen.

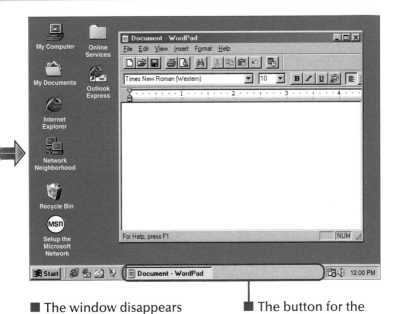

■ The window disappears from your screen.

■ The button for the window disappears from the taskbar.

SHOW THE DESKTOP

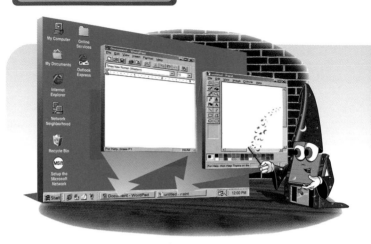

SHOW THE DESKTOP

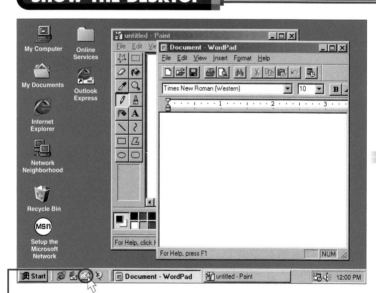

1 To minimize all the open windows on your screen, move the mouse ⌖ over 🖳 and then press the left button.

24

You can instantly minimize all your open windows to remove them from your screen. This allows you to clearly view the desktop.

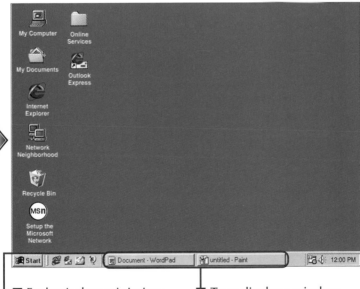

■ Each window minimizes to a button on the taskbar. You can now clearly view the desktop.

■ To redisplay a window, move the mouse ⇧ over its button on the taskbar and then press the left button.

SHUT DOWN WINDOWS

When you finish using your computer, you should shut down Windows before turning off the computer.

SHUT DOWN WINDOWS

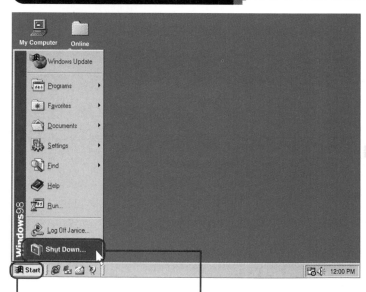

1 Move the mouse ⌖ over **Start** and then press the left button.

2 Move the mouse ⌖ over **Shut Down** and then press the left button.

■ The Shut Down Windows dialog box appears.

■ Do not turn off your computer until this message appears on your screen.

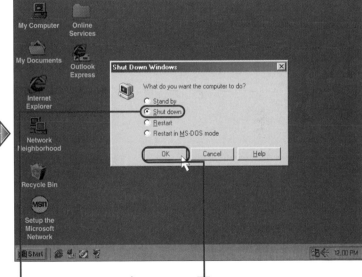

3 Move the mouse ⌖ over **Shut down** and then press the left button (○ changes to ⊙).

4 To shut down your computer, move the mouse ⌖ over **OK** and then press the left button.

27

GETTING HELP

GETTING HELP

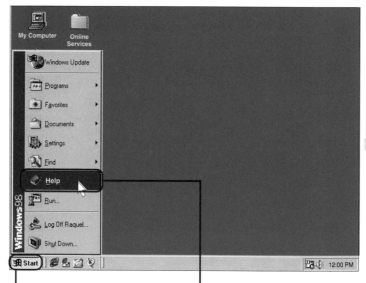

1 Move the mouse ⍟ over **Start** and then press the left button.

2 Move the mouse ⍟ over **Help** and then press the left button.

■ The Windows Help window appears.

If you do not
know how to perform a
task, you can use the
Help feature to get
information.

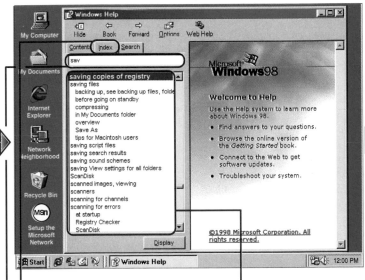

3 To display an alphabetical list of help topics, move the mouse ⬚ over the **Index** tab and then press the left button.

4 Move the mouse ⬚ over this area and then press the left button. Type the first few letters of the topic of interest.

■ This area displays help topics beginning with the letters you typed.

CONTINUED

29

GETTING HELP

GETTING HELP (CONTINUED)

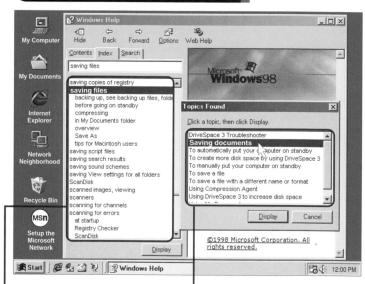

5 Move the mouse ⌖ over the help topic you want information on and then quickly press the left button twice.

■ The Topics Found dialog box may appear, displaying a list of related help topics.

6 Move the mouse ⌖ over the help topic of interest and then quickly press the left button twice.

The Help feature can save you time by eliminating the need to refer to other sources.

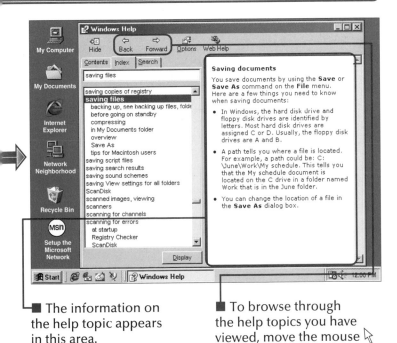

■ The information on the help topic appears in this area.

■ To browse through the help topics you have viewed, move the mouse over **Back** or **Forward** and then press the left button.

START WORDPAD

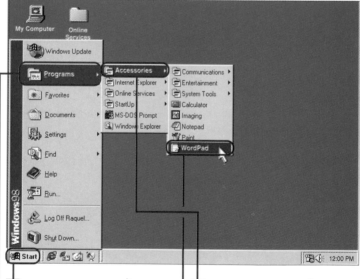

1 Move the mouse ⩗ over **Start** and then press the left button.

2 Move the mouse ⩗ over **Programs**.

3 Move the mouse ⩗ over **Accessories**.

4 Move the mouse ⩗ over **WordPad** and then press the left button.

32

WordPad allows you to create simple documents, such as letters and memos.

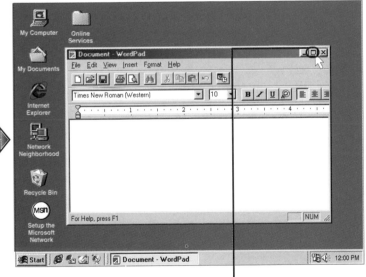

■ The WordPad window appears with a new, blank document.

5 To enlarge the WordPad window to fill your screen, move the mouse over ⬜ and then press the left button.

33

ENTER TEXT

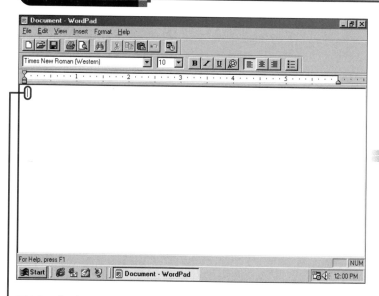

The flashing line on your screen, called the insertion point, indicates where the text you type will appear.

When typing text in a document, you do not need to press the Enter key at the end of a line. WordPad automatically moves the text to the next line.

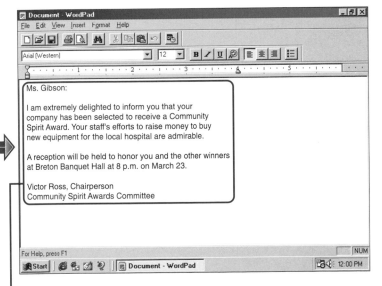

1 Type the text for your document.

■ Press the Enter key only when you want to start a new line or paragraph.

Note: To make the example easier to read, the font type and size have been changed. To change the font type, see page 48. To change the font size, see page 50.

35

INSERT TEXT

INSERT TEXT

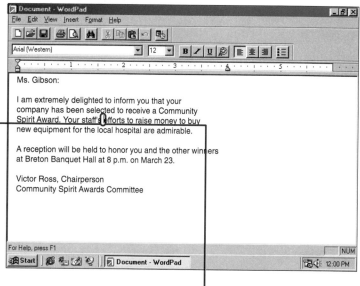

Document - WordPad

File   Edit   View   Insert   Format   Help

Arial (Western)   12   **B** / U 🖉 📰 📄 📄 📄

Ms. Gibson:

I am extremely delighted to inform you that your
company has been selected to receive a Community
Spirit Award. Your staff's efforts to raise money to buy
new equipment for the local hospital are admirable.

A reception will be held to honor you and the other winners
at Breton Banquet Hall at 8 p.m. on March 23.

Victor Ross, Chairperson
Community Spirit Awards Committee

For Help, press F1   NUM

Start | | Document - WordPad   12:00 PM

1 Move the mouse I
over the location where
you want to insert text
and then press the left
button.

■ The flashing insertion
point indicates where the
text you type will appear.

You can easily add new text to your document.

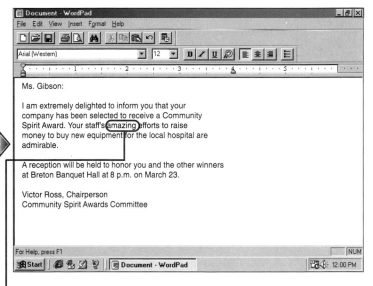

2 Type the text you want to insert.

3 To insert a blank space, press the Spacebar.

Note: The words to the right of the new text move forward.

DELETE TEXT

DELETE TEXT

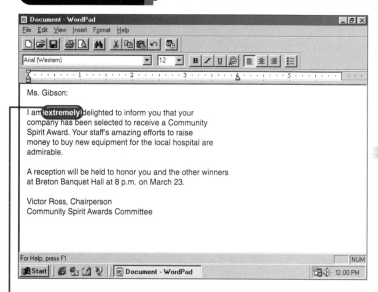

1 To select the text you want to delete, press and hold down the left button as you drag the mouse I over the text until the text is highlighted.

You can easily remove text that you no longer need in your document.

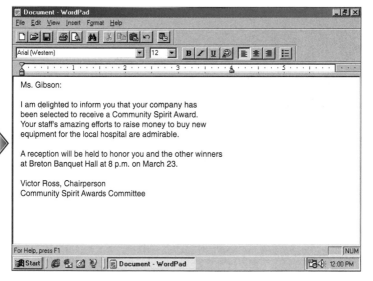

2 Press the Delete key to remove the text.

■ To delete one character at a time, move the mouse I to the left of the first character you want to delete and then press the left button. Press the Delete key for each character you want to remove.

SAVE A DOCUMENT

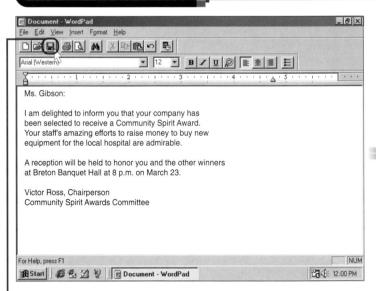

1 To save the document, move the mouse ⬚ over 🖫 and then press the left button.

■ The Save As dialog box appears.

Note: If you previously saved the document, the Save As dialog box will not appear since you have already named the document.

You should save your document to store it for future use. This lets you later retrieve the document for reviewing or editing.

You should regularly save changes you make to a document to avoid losing your work.

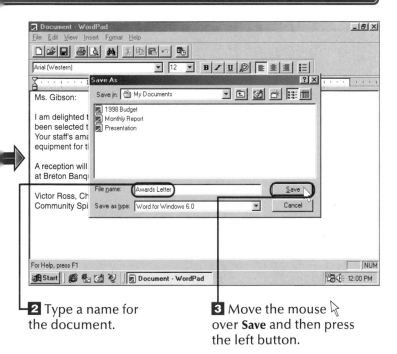

2 Type a name for the document.

3 Move the mouse � over **Save** and then press the left button.

41

PRINT A DOCUMENT

PRINT A DOCUMENT

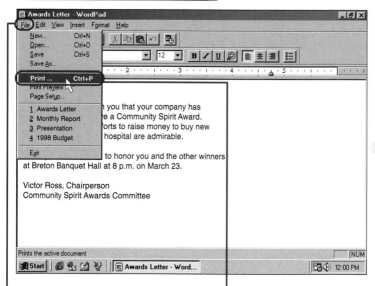

1 Move the mouse ⟨ over **File** and then press the left button.

2 Move the mouse ⟨ over **Print** and then press the left button.

You can produce a paper copy of the document displayed on your screen.

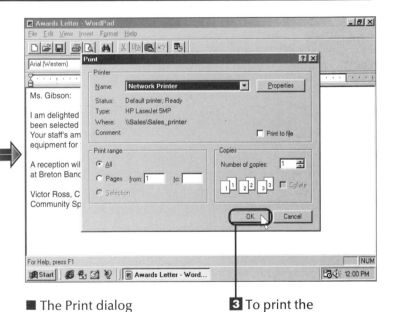

■ The Print dialog box appears.

3 To print the document, move the mouse ⟍ over **OK** and then press the left button.

43

OPEN A
DOCUMENT

OPEN A DOCUMENT

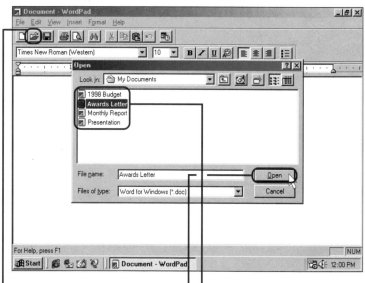

1 To open a document, move the mouse ⟍ over 🗁 and then press the left button.

■ The Open dialog box appears.

2 Move the mouse ⟍ over the name of the document you want to open and then press the left button.

3 Move the mouse ⟍ over **Open** and then press the left button.

44

You can open a saved document and display the document on your screen. This allows you to view and make changes to the document.

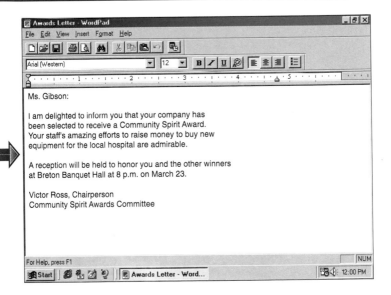

■ WordPad opens the document and displays it on your screen. You can now review and make changes to the document.

QUICKLY OPEN A DOCUMENT

QUICKLY OPEN A DOCUMENT

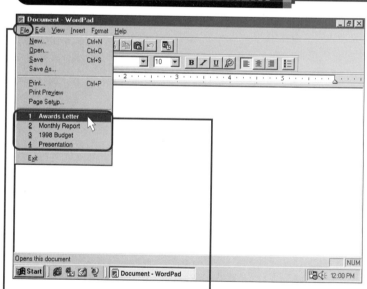

1 To quickly open a document, move the mouse ⌖ over **File** and then press the left button.

2 Move the mouse ⌖ over the name of the document you want to open and then press the left button.

The File menu displays the names of the last four documents you opened. You can quickly open one of these documents.

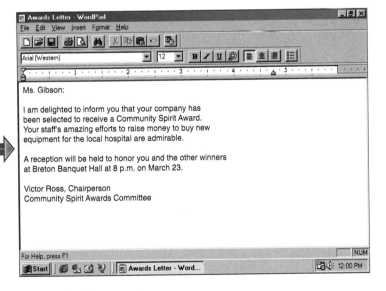

■ WordPad opens the document and displays it on your screen. You can now review and make changes to the document.

CHANGE FONT TYPE

CHANGE FONT TYPE

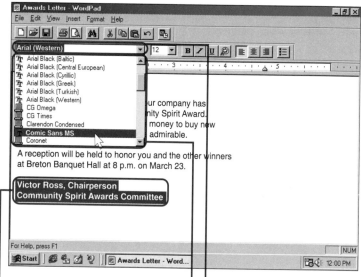

1 To select the text you want to change to a new font type, press and hold down the left button as you drag the mouse I over the text until the text is highlighted.

2 To display a list of the available font types, move the mouse $\diagdown$ over ▼ in this area and then press the left button.

3 Move the mouse $\diagdown$ over the font type you want to use and then press the left button.

You can enhance
the appearance of your
document by changing
the design of
the text.

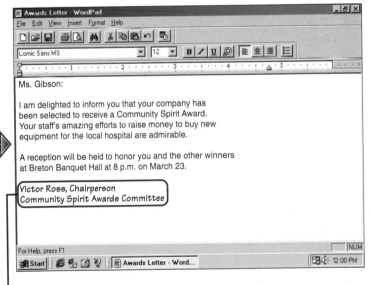

■ The text you
selected changes to
the new font type.

■ To deselect text, move
the mouse I outside the
selected area and then
press the left button.

49

CHANGE FONT SIZE

CHANGE FONT SIZE

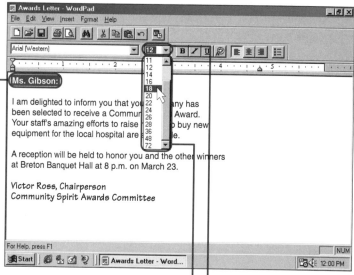

1 To select the text you want to change to a new font size, press and hold down the left button as you drag the mouse ⌶ over the text until the text is highlighted.

2 To display a list of the available font sizes, move the mouse ⌖ over ▼ in this area and then press the left button.

3 Move the mouse ⌖ over the font size you want to use and then press the left button.

You can increase or decrease the size of text in your document.

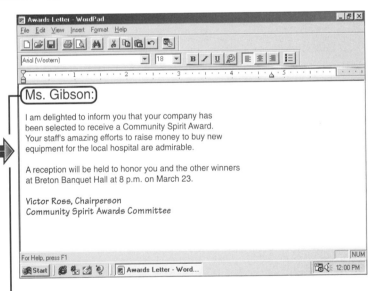

■ The text you selected changes to the new font size.

■ To deselect text, move the mouse I outside the selected area and then press the left button.

BOLD, ITALIC AND UNDERLINE

BOLD, ITALIC AND UNDERLINE

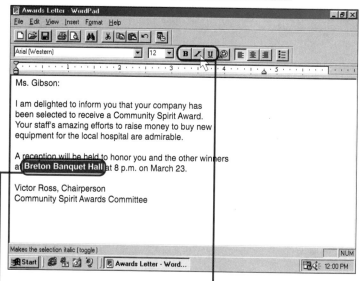

1 To select the text you want to change to a new style, press and hold down the left button as you drag the mouse I over the text until the text is highlighted.

2 Move the mouse ⍾ over one of the following styles and then press the left button.

B Bold

I Italic

U̲ Underline

You can use the
Bold, Italic and Underline
features to emphasize
important information
in your document.

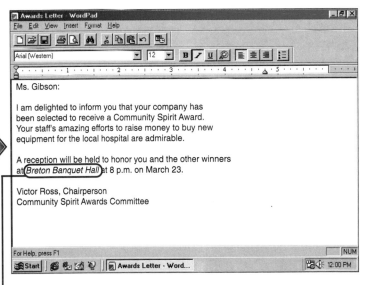

■ The text you selected
appears in the new style.

■ To deselect text, move
the mouse I outside the
selected area and then
press the left button.

■ To remove a bold, italic
or underline style, repeat
steps 1 and 2.

53

CHANGE ALIGNMENT OF TEXT

CHANGE ALIGNMENT OF TEXT

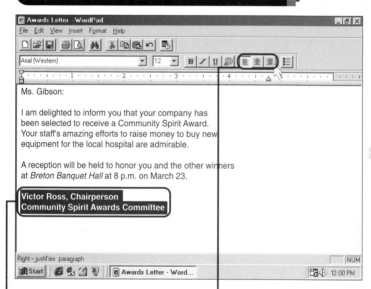

Ms. Gibson:

I am delighted to inform you that your company has been selected to receive a Community Spirit Award. Your staff's amazing efforts to raise money to buy new equipment for the local hospital are admirable.

A reception will be held to honor you and the other winners at *Breton Banquet Hall* at 8 p.m. on March 23.

Victor Ross, Chairperson
Community Spirit Awards Committee

Right – justifies paragraph

1 To select the text you want to align differently, press and hold down the left button as you drag the mouse I over the text until the text is highlighted.

2 Move the mouse ⇗ over one of the following options and then press the left button.

▤ Left align

▤ Center

▤ Right align

You can make
your document look
more attractive by
aligning text in
different ways.

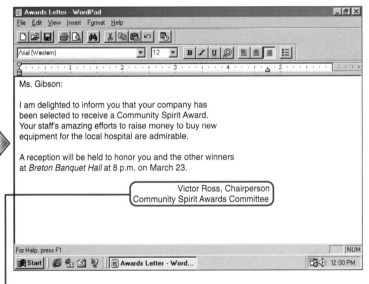

■ The text displays the
new alignment.

■ To deselect text, move
the mouse I outside the
selected area and then
press the left button.

55

START PAINT

START PAINT

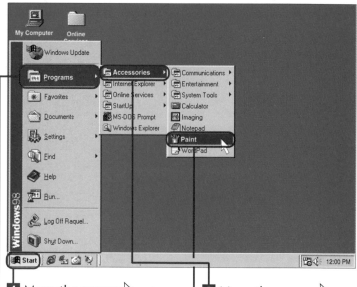

1 Move the mouse ⌖ over **Start** and then press the left button.

2 Move the mouse ⌖ over **Programs**.

3 Move the mouse ⌖ over **Accessories**.

4 Move the mouse ⌖ over **Paint** and then press the left button.

You can use
Paint to draw pictures
and maps on your
computer.

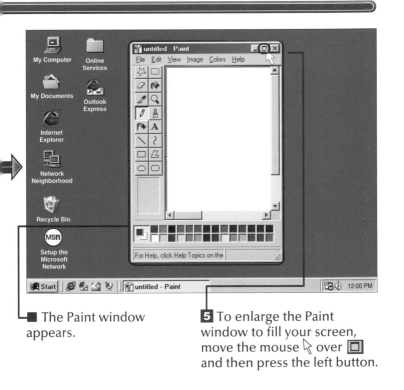

■ The Paint window
appears.

5 To enlarge the Paint
window to fill your screen,
move the mouse ⬚ over □
and then press the left button.

DRAW SHAPES

You can draw shapes to create a picture. Paint offers three options for drawing shapes.

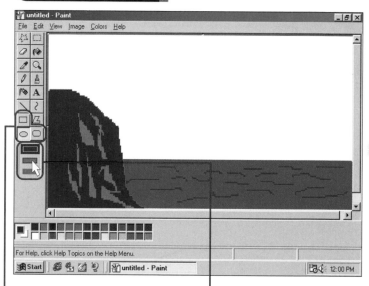

1 Move the mouse ⌖ over the tool for the type of shape you want to draw (example: ⬭) and then press the left button.

2 To select how you want to draw the shape, move the mouse ⌖ over one of the options in this area and then press the left button.

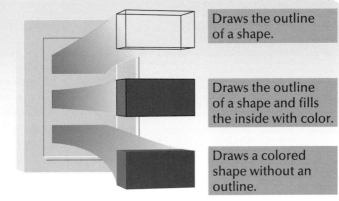

Draws the outline of a shape.

Draws the outline of a shape and fills the inside with color.

Draws a colored shape without an outline.

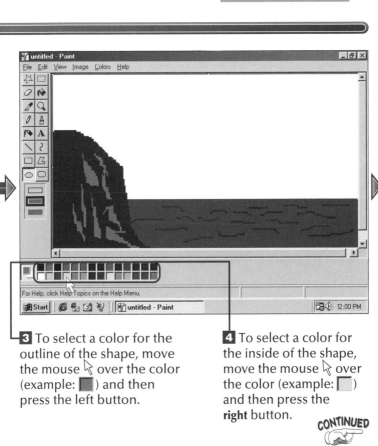

3 To select a color for the outline of the shape, move the mouse ⬉ over the color (example: ■) and then press the left button.

4 To select a color for the inside of the shape, move the mouse ⬉ over the color (example: ☐) and then press the **right** button.

CONTINUED

59

DRAW SHAPES

DRAW SHAPES (CONTINUED)

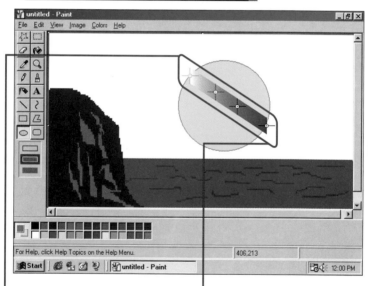

5 Position the mouse ⤢ where you want to begin drawing the shape (⤢ changes to ✛).

6 Press and hold down the left button as you drag the mouse ✛ until the shape is the size you want.

Note: To draw a perfect circle or square, press and hold down the **Shift** *key as you perform step* **6**.

60

You can use Paint's tools to draw shapes such as circles, squares and rectangles.

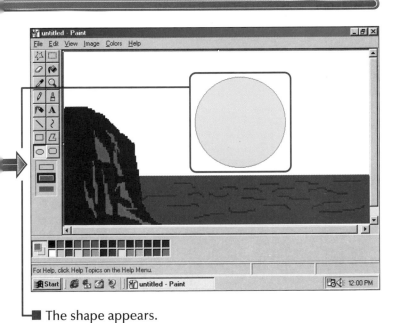

■ The shape appears.

DRAW LINES

Paint lets you draw several types of lines in various colors.

DRAW LINES

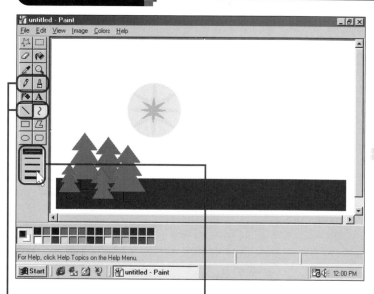

1 Move the mouse ▷ over the tool for the type of line you want to draw (example: ❨) and then press the left button.

2 To select a line thickness, move the mouse ▷ over one of the options in this area and then press the left button.

Note: The ✐ tool does not provide any line thickness options. The ▤ tool provides a different set of options.

	Draws thin, wavy lines.
	Draws wavy lines of different thicknesses.
	Draws straight lines of different thicknesses.
	Draws curved lines of different thicknesses.

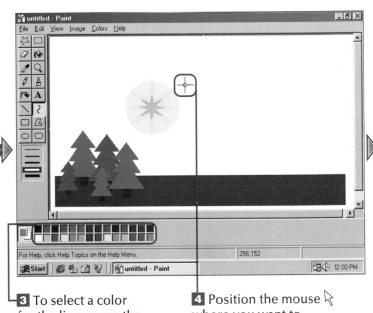

3 To select a color for the line, move the mouse ⌖ over the color (example: ■) and then press the left button.

4 Position the mouse ⌖ where you want to begin drawing the line (⌖ changes to ⊹, 𝕡 or ┼).

CONTINUED

63

DRAW LINES

DRAW LINES (CONTINUED)

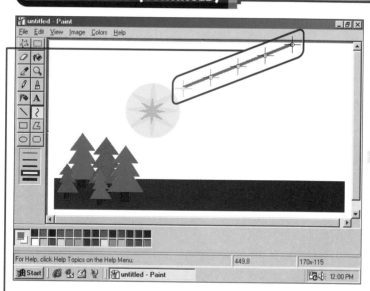

5 Press and hold down the left button as you drag the mouse ⟡ until the line is the length you want.

Note: When using the ＼ or 𝟉 tool, you can draw a perfectly horizontal, vertical or 45-degree line. To do so, press and hold down the Shift key as you perform step 5.

64

Like painting on canvas, you can use the mouse to draw lines in your picture.

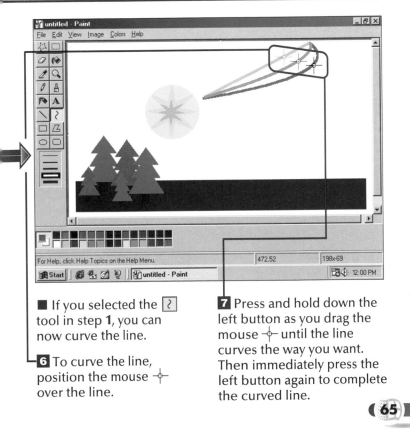

■ If you selected the [curve] tool in step **1**, you can now curve the line.

6 To curve the line, position the mouse ⊹ over the line.

7 Press and hold down the left button as you drag the mouse ⊹ until the line curves the way you want. Then immediately press the left button again to complete the curved line.

65

ADD TEXT

1 To add text to your picture, move the mouse ⟍ over **A** and then press the left button.

2 To select a color for the text, move the mouse ⟍ over a color (example: ■) and then press the left button.

You can add text to your picture, such as a title or explanation.

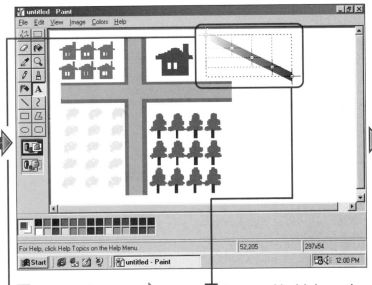

3 Position the mouse ⊹ where you want to display the top left edge of the text (⊹ changes to ⊹).

4 Press and hold down the left button as you drag the mouse ⊹ to select the area where you want the text to appear.

■ A dotted box appears.

CONTINUED

67

ADD TEXT (CONTINUED)

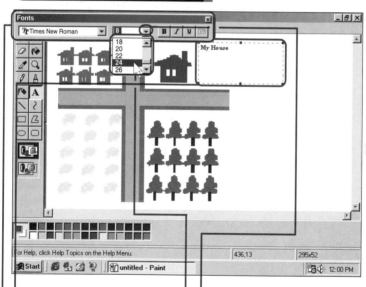

5 Type the text you want to add to the picture.

■ The Text Toolbar lets you change the size of the text.

6 To change the size of the text, move the mouse ▷ over ▼ in this area and then press the left button.

7 Move the mouse ▷ over the size you want to use and then press the left button.

When adding
text to a picture, you
can use the Text Toolbar
to change the size of
the text.

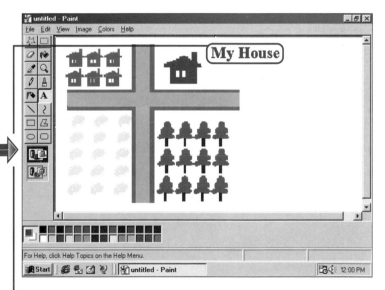

■ The text appears in the
new size.

8 When you finish changing
the text, move the mouse ⊹
outside the text box and then
press the left button.

*Note: After you perform
step 8, you can no longer
edit or change the
appearance of the text.*

69

ERASE PART OF A PICTURE

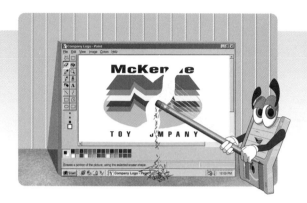

ERASE PART OF A PICTURE

Erases a portion of the picture, using the selected eraser shape.

1 Move the mouse ⌖ over ⬜ and then press the left button.

2 Move the mouse ⌖ over the size of eraser you want to use and then press the left button.

3 Move the mouse ⌖ over a color for the eraser (example: ⬜) and then press the **right** button.

70

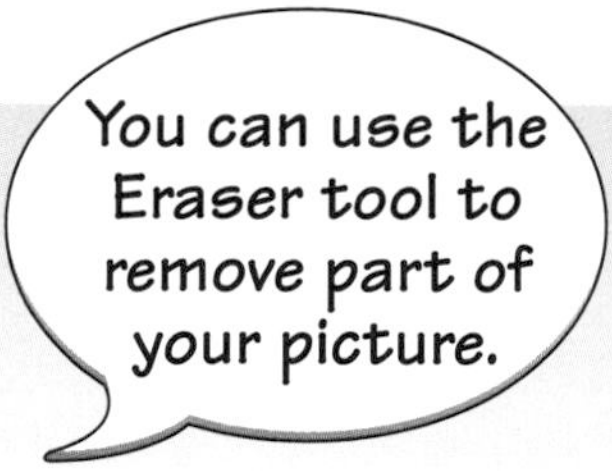

You can use the Eraser tool to remove part of your picture.

When choosing a color for the eraser, select a color that matches the background color of your picture.

4 Position the mouse � where you want to start erasing (� changes to ☐).

5 Press and hold down the left button as you drag the mouse ☐ over the area you want to erase.

Note: To immediately undo the change, press and hold down the **Ctrl** *key and then press the* **Z** *key.*

71

SAVE A PICTURE

SAVE A PICTURE

1 Move the mouse ⟍ over **File** and then press the left button.

2 Move the mouse ⟍ over **Save** and then press the left button.

■ The Save As dialog box appears.

Note: If you previously saved the picture, the Save As dialog box will not appear since you have already named the picture.

You should save your picture to store the picture for future use. This lets you later review and make changes to the picture.

You should regularly save changes you make to a picture to avoid losing your work.

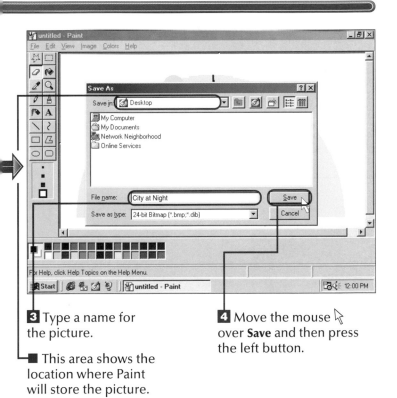

3 Type a name for the picture.

■ This area shows the location where Paint will store the picture.

4 Move the mouse ⌖ over **Save** and then press the left button.

OPEN A PICTURE

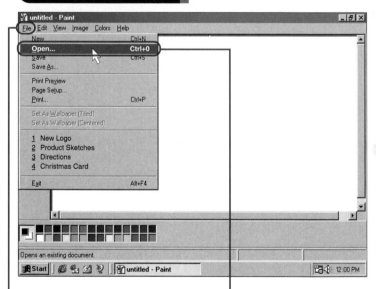

1 Move the mouse ☐ over **File** and then press the left button.

2 Move the mouse ☐ over **Open** and then press the left button.

■ The Open dialog box appears.

You can open a
saved picture and display
the picture on your screen.
This allows you to view
and make changes
to the picture.

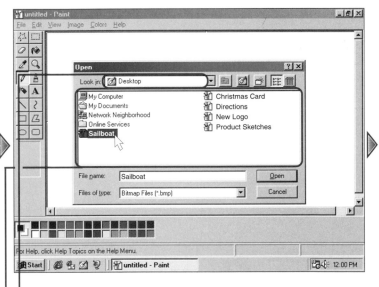

■ This area shows the
location of the displayed
pictures.

*Note: If you cannot find the
picture you want to open, see
page 118 to find the picture.*

3 Move the mouse ⃕ over
the name of the picture
you want to open and
then press the left button.

CONTINUED

75

OPEN A PICTURE

OPEN A PICTURE (CONTINUED)

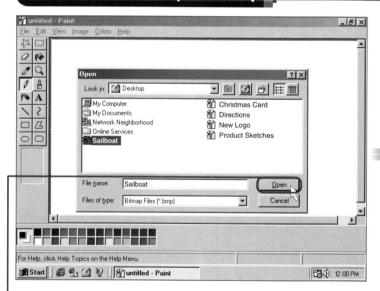

4 Move the mouse over **Open** and then press the left button.

76

Paint lets you work with only one picture at a time. When you open a picture, Paint closes the picture you are currently working with.

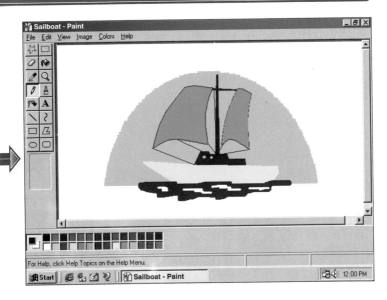

■ Paint opens the picture and displays it on your screen. You can now review and make changes to the picture.

QUICKLY OPEN A PICTURE

QUICKLY OPEN A PICTURE

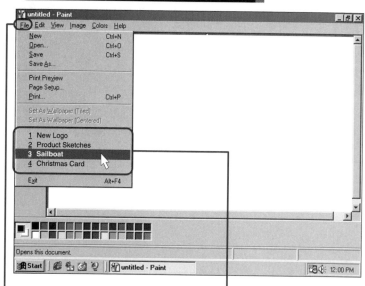

1 Move the mouse ⌖ over **File** and then press the left button.

2 Move the mouse ⌖ over the name of the picture you want to open and then press the left button.

78

The File menu displays the names of the last four pictures you opened. You can quickly open one of these pictures.

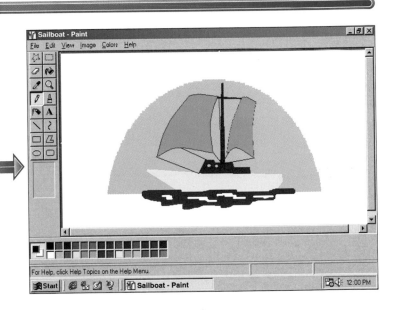

■ Paint opens the picture and displays it on your screen. You can now review and make changes to the picture.

79

VIEW CONTENTS OF YOUR COMPUTER

VIEW CONTENTS OF YOUR COMPUTER

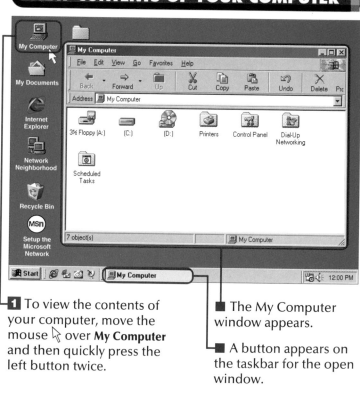

1 To view the contents of your computer, move the mouse ↖ over **My Computer** and then quickly press the left button twice.

■ The My Computer window appears.

■ A button appears on the taskbar for the open window.

80

You can easily view the folders and files stored on your computer.

Like a filing cabinet, your computer uses folders to organize information.

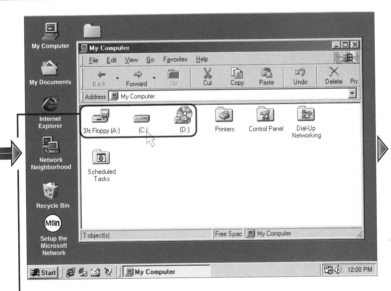

These items represent the drives on your computer.

2 To display the contents of a drive, move the mouse ⬚ over the drive and then quickly press the left button twice.

Note: If you want to view the contents of a floppy or CD-ROM drive, make sure you insert a floppy disk or CD-ROM disc before performing step 2.

CONTINUED

81

Windows Icons

Folder

Program

Paint

WordPad

VIEW CONTENTS (CONTINUED)

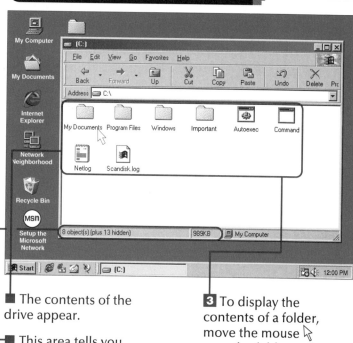

■ The contents of the drive appear.

■ This area tells you how many items are in the window and the total size of the items.

3 To display the contents of a folder, move the mouse ⌖ over the folder and then quickly press the left button twice.

82

Each item in a window displays a symbol to help you distinguish between the different types of items.

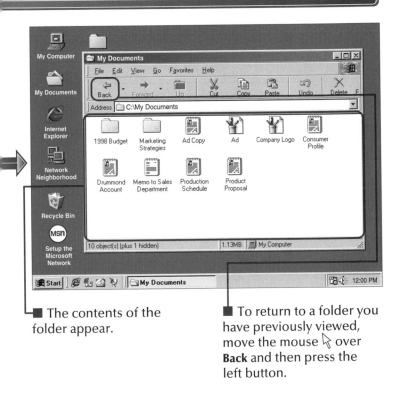

■ The contents of the folder appear.

■ To return to a folder you have previously viewed, move the mouse ⬉ over **Back** and then press the left button.

83

CHANGE APPEARANCE OF ITEMS

CHANGE APPEARANCE OF ITEMS

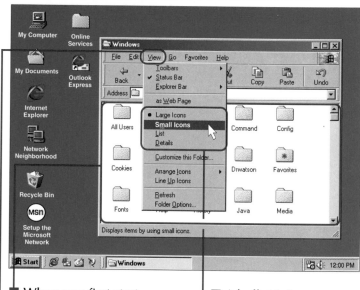

■ When you first start using Windows, items are displayed as large icons.

1 To change the appearance of items, move the mouse ⃗ over **View** and then press the left button.

■ A bullet (●) appears beside the way the items are currently displayed.

2 Move the mouse ⃗ over the way you want to display the items and then press the left button.

84

You can change the appearance of items in a window. Items can appear as large icons, small icons or in a list. You can also display details about each item.

An icon is a picture that represents an item such as a file, folder or program.

In this example, the items are displayed as small icons.

SORT ITEMS

NAME — SORT ITEMS
SIZE — SORT ITEMS
TYPE — SORT ITEMS
DATE — SORT ITEMS

SORT ITEMS

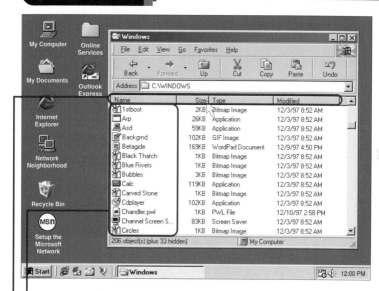

■ When you first start using Windows, items are sorted alphabetically by name.

Note: If the headings are not displayed, perform steps 1 and 2 on page 84, selecting Details in step 2.

1 Move the mouse ⟍ over the heading for the column you want to use to sort the items and then press the left button.

You can sort the items displayed in a window. This can help you find files and folders more easily.

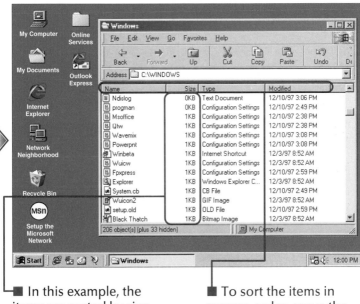

■ In this example, the items are sorted by size from smallest to largest.

■ To sort the items in reverse order, move the mouse ⍗ over the heading again and then press the left button.

87

ARRANGE ITEMS AUTOMATICALLY

ARRANGE ITEMS AUTOMATICALLY

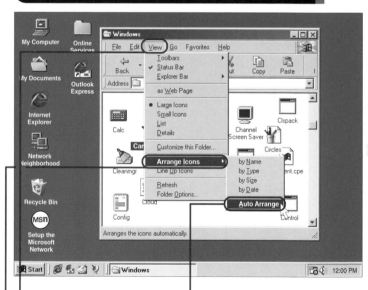

1 Move the mouse ⟋ over **View** and then press the left button.

2 Move the mouse ⟋ over **Arrange Icons**.

■ A check mark (✔) appears beside Auto Arrange when this feature is on.

3 To turn this feature on, move the mouse ⟋ over **Auto Arrange** and then press the left button.

You can have Windows automatically arrange items to fit neatly in a window.

The Auto Arrange feature is not available when items appear in the List or Details view. To change the view, see page 84.

■ The items are automatically arranged in the window.

■ To turn off the Auto Arrange feature, repeat steps 1 to 3.

■ When you change the size of a window and the Auto Arrange feature is on, Windows automatically rearranges the items to fit the new window size.

Note: To size a window, see page 16.

89

OPEN A FILE

OPEN A FILE

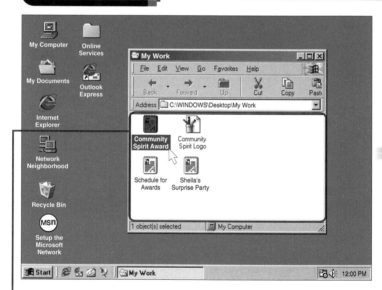

1 Move the mouse ⬚ over the file you want to open and then quickly press the left button twice.

90

You can open a file to display its contents on your screen. This lets you review and make changes to the file.

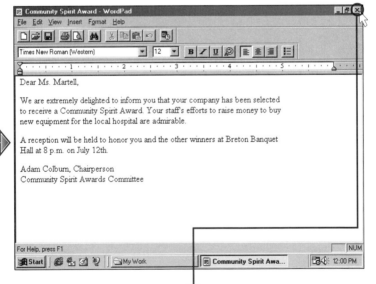

■ The file opens. You can review and make changes to the file.

2 When you finish working with the file, move the mouse ↖ over ☒ and then press the left button.

OPEN A RECENTLY USED FILE

OPEN A RECENTLY USED FILE

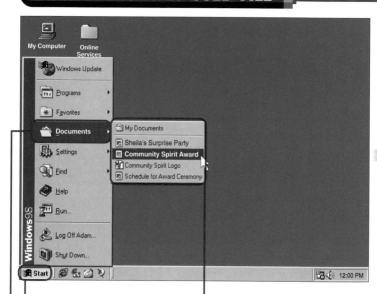

1 Move the mouse ⊹ over **Start** and then press the left button.

2 Move the mouse ⊹ over **Documents**.

3 Move the mouse ⊹ over the file you want to open and then press the left button.

*Note: The My Documents folder stores many documents you have created. To open the folder, move the mouse ⊹ over **My Documents** and then press the left button.*

92

Windows remembers the files you most recently used. You can quickly open any of these files.

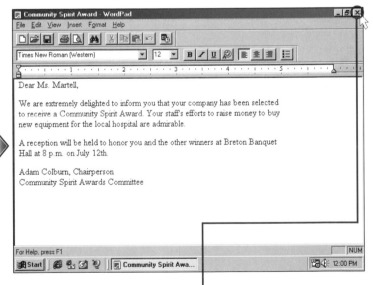

■ The file opens. You can review and make changes to the file.

4 When you finish working with the file, move the mouse ⌖ over ✕ and then press the left button.

SELECT FILES

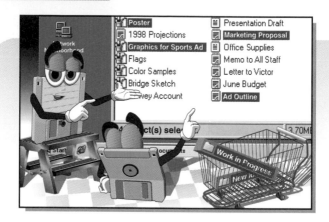

SELECT A FILE

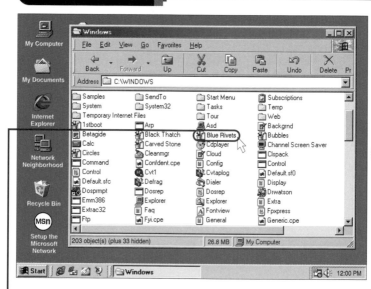

1 Move the mouse ⬚ over the file you want to select and then press the left button.

Note: You can select a folder the same way you select a file. Selecting a folder will select all the files in the folder.

Before working
with files, you must first
select the files you want
to work with. Selected
files appear highlighted
on your screen.

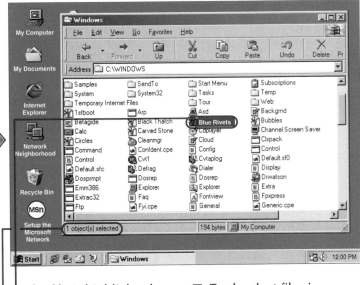

■ The file is highlighted.

└─ ■ This area displays
the number of files
you selected.

■ To deselect files in
a window, move the
mouse ⬆ over a blank
area in the window
and then press
the left button.

CONTINUED

95

SELECT FILES

SELECT MULTIPLE FILES

My Computer

My Documents

Internet Explorer

Network Neighborhood

Recycle Bin

MSN

Setup the Microsoft Network

Windows

File   Edit   View   Go   Favorites   Help

Back   Forward   Up   Cut   Copy   Paste   Undo   Delete   Pr

Address 🗀 C:\WINDOWS

Samples	SendTo	Start Menu	Subscriptions
System	System32	Tasks	Temp
Temporary Internet Files	Tour	Web	
1stboot	Arp	Asd	Backgrnd
Betagide	Black Thatch	**Blue Rivets**	Bubbles
Calc	Carved Stone	**Cdplayer**	Channel Screen Saver
Circles	Cleanmgr	**Cloud**	Clspack
Command	Confdent.cpe	**Config**	Control
Control	Cvt1	**Cvtaplog**	Default.sf0
Default.sfc	Defrag	**Dialer**	Display
Dosprmpt	Dosrep	**Dosrep**	Drwatson
Emm386	Explorer	**Explorer**	Extra
Extrac32	Faq	General	Fpxpress
Ftp	Fyi.cpe		Generic.cpe

8 object(s) selected   267KB   🖳 My Computer

🏁 Start   Windows   12:00 PM

SELECT A GROUP OF FILES

1 Move the mouse ⍅ over the first file you want to select and then press the left button.

2 Press and hold down the Shift key.

3 Still holding down the Shift key, move the mouse ⍅ over the last file you want to select and then press the left button.

You can select
multiple files. This
lets you work with
several files at the
same time.

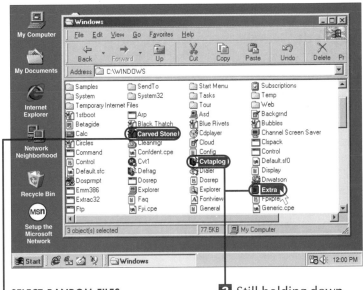

SELECT RANDOM FILES

1 Move the mouse over a file you want to select and then press the left button.

2 Press and hold down the Ctrl key.

3 Still holding down the Ctrl key, move the mouse over each file you want to select and then press the left button.

97

RENAME A FILE

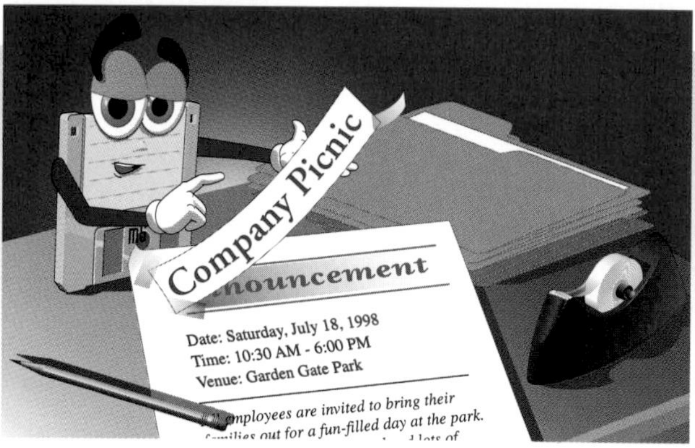

RENAME A FILE

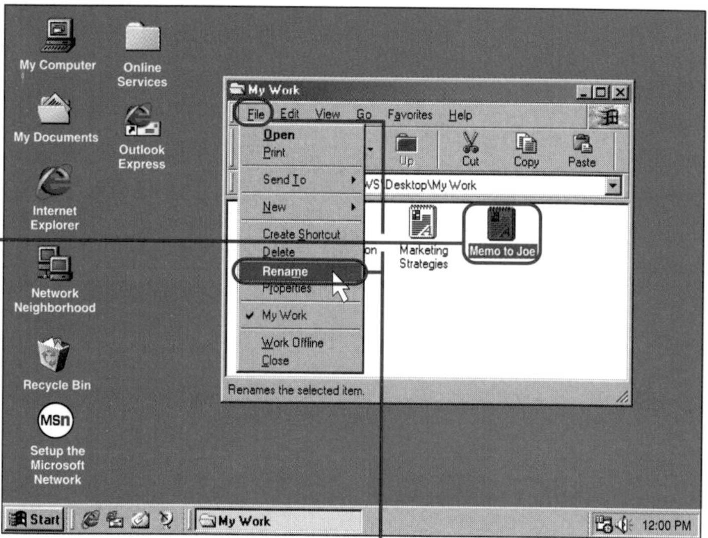

1 Move the mouse over the file you want to rename and then press the left button.

2 Move the mouse over **File** and then press the left button.

3 Move the mouse over **Rename** and then press the left button.

> You can give a file a new name to better describe the contents of the file. This can make the file easier to find.

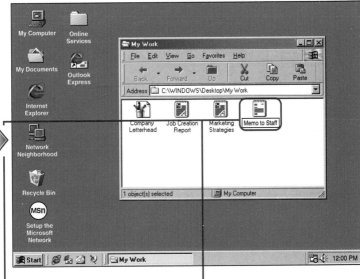

■ The name of the file appears in a box.

4 Type a new name for the file and then press the **Enter** key.

*Note: You can use up to 255 characters to name a file. The name cannot contain the \ / : * ? " < > or | characters.*

99

CREATE A NEW FOLDER

CREATE A NEW FOLDER

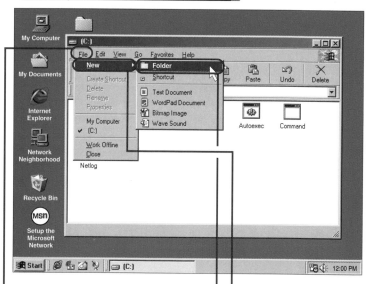

1 Display the contents of the folder where you want to place the new folder.

2 Move the mouse ⌖ over **File** and then press the left button.

3 Move the mouse ⌖ over **New**.

4 Move the mouse ⌖ over **Folder** and then press the left button.

You can create a new folder to help you better organize the information stored on your computer.

Creating a folder is like placing a new folder in a filing cabinet.

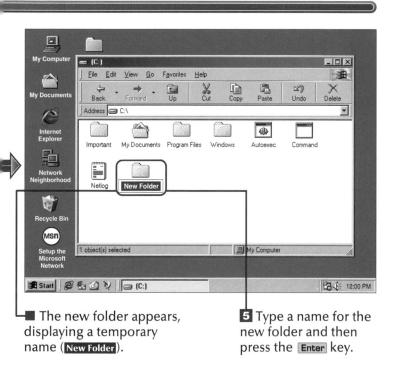

■ The new folder appears, displaying a temporary name (New Folder).

5 Type a name for the new folder and then press the **Enter** key.

101

MOVE FILES

MOVE FILES

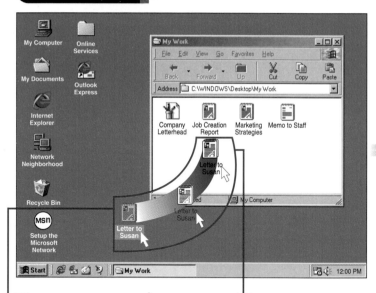

1 Position the mouse ⤢ over the file you want to move.

Note: To move more than one file, select all the files you want to move. Then position the mouse ⤢ over one of the files. To select multiple files, see page 96.

2 Press and hold down the left button as you drag the file to a new location on your computer.

You can organize
the files stored on your
computer by moving them
to new locations.

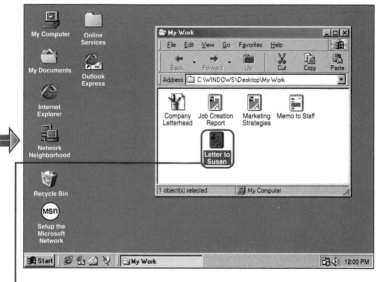

■ The file moves to
the new location.

*Note: You can move folders the
same way you move files. When
you move a folder, all the files in
the folder also move.*

COPY FILES

COPY FILES

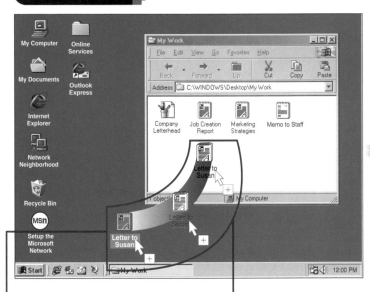

1 Position the mouse ⌖ over the file you want to copy.

2 Press and hold down the Ctrl key.

3 Still holding down the Ctrl key, press and hold down the left button as you drag the file to a new location.

You can make
an exact copy of a file
and then place the copy
in a new location. This
lets you store the file
in two locations.

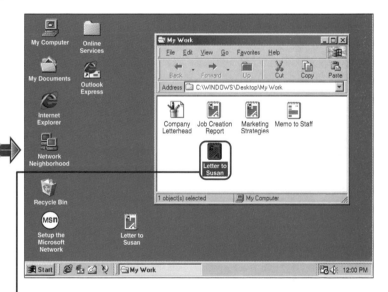

■ A copy of the file
appears in the new
location.

*Note: You can copy folders the
same way you copy files. When
you copy a folder, all the files in
the folder are also copied.*

105

COPY A FILE TO A FLOPPY DISK

COPY A FILE TO A FLOPPY DISK

1 Insert a floppy disk into a drive.

2 Move the mouse ⟍ over the file you want to copy and then press the left button.

Note: To copy more than one file, select all the files you want to copy. To select multiple files, see page 96.

106

You can place a copy of a file on a floppy disk. This is useful if you want to give a colleague a copy of the file.

You can copy folders the same way you copy files. When you copy a folder, all the files in the folder are also copied.

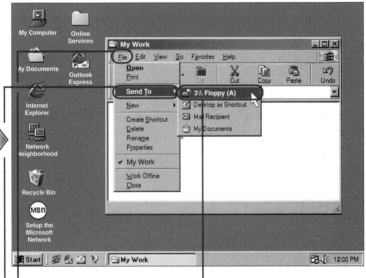

3 Move the mouse ⬉ over **File** and then press the left button.

4 Move the mouse ⬉ over **Send To**.

5 Move the mouse ⬉ over the drive where you want to place a copy of the file and then press the left button.

■ Windows places a copy of the file on the floppy disk.

107

DELETE A FILE

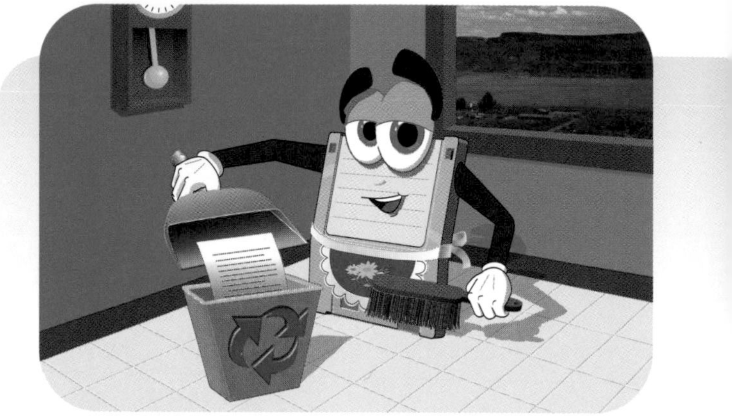

DELETE A FILE

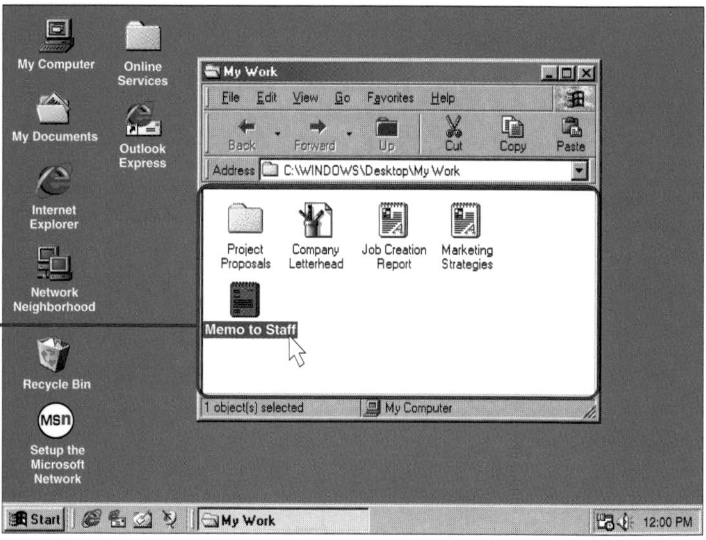

1 Move the mouse over the file you want to delete and then press the left button.

Note: To delete more than one file, select the files. To select multiple files, see page 96.

You can delete a file you no longer need.

Before you delete any files you have created, consider the value of your work. Do not delete a file unless you are certain you no longer need the file.

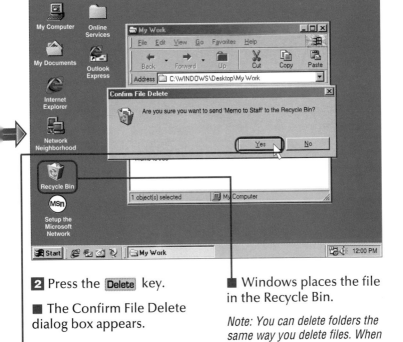

2 Press the Delete key.

■ The Confirm File Delete dialog box appears.

3 To delete the file, move the mouse ⬚ over **Yes** and then press the left button.

■ Windows places the file in the Recycle Bin.

Note: You can delete folders the same way you delete files. When you delete a folder, all the files in the folder are also deleted.

109

RESTORE A DELETED FILE

RESTORE A DELETED FILE

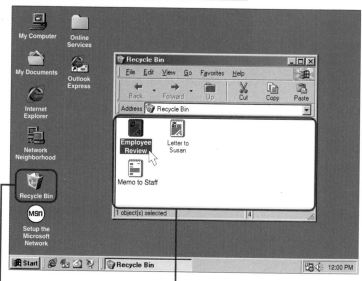

1 Move the mouse ⌖ over **Recycle Bin** and then quickly press the left button twice.

■ The Recycle Bin window appears, displaying all the files you have deleted.

2 Move the mouse ⌖ over the file you want to restore and then press the left button.

110

The Recycle Bin stores all the files you have deleted. You can easily restore any of these files.

You can restore folders the same way you restore files. When you restore a folder, all the files in the folder are also restored.

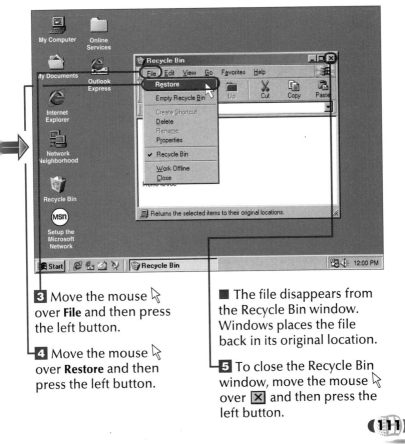

3 Move the mouse ⤢ over **File** and then press the left button.

4 Move the mouse ⤢ over **Restore** and then press the left button.

■ The file disappears from the Recycle Bin window. Windows places the file back in its original location.

5 To close the Recycle Bin window, move the mouse ⤢ over ✕ and then press the left button.

111

EMPTY THE RECYCLE BIN

EMPTY THE RECYCLE BIN

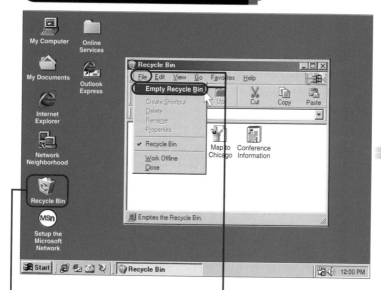

1 Move the mouse ⌖ over **Recycle Bin** and then quickly press the left button twice.

■ The Recycle Bin window appears, displaying all the files you have deleted.

2 Move the mouse ⌖ over **File** and then press the left button.

3 Move the mouse ⌖ over **Empty Recycle Bin** and then press the left button.

You can create
more free space on your
computer by permanently
removing all the files from
the Recycle Bin.

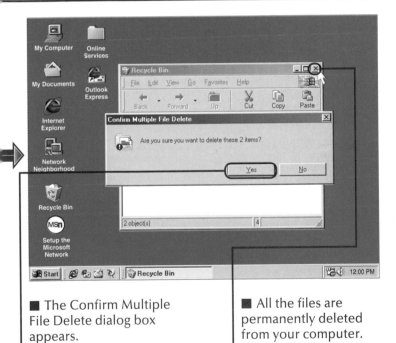

■ The Confirm Multiple
File Delete dialog box
appears.

4 To permanently
delete all the files, move
the mouse ⇧ over **Yes**
and then press the left
button.

■ All the files are
permanently deleted
from your computer.

5 To close the Recycle
Bin window, move the
mouse ⇧ over **☒** and
then press the left
button.

113

PRINT A FILE

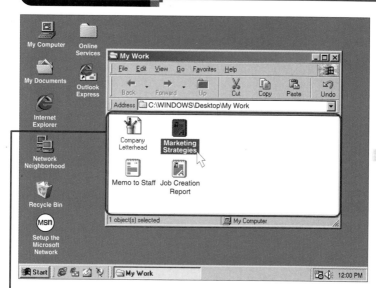

1 Move the mouse ⬚ over the file you want to print and then press the left button.

Note: To print more than one file, select the files. To select multiple files, see page 96.

You can produce a paper copy of a file stored on your computer.

Before printing, make sure your printer is turned on and contains paper.

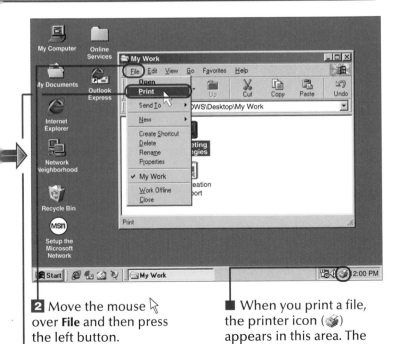

2 Move the mouse ⌖ over **File** and then press the left button.

3 Move the mouse ⌖ over **Print** and then press the left button.

■ When you print a file, the printer icon (🖨) appears in this area. The icon disappears when the file has finished printing.

115

CANCEL PRINTING

CANCEL PRINTING

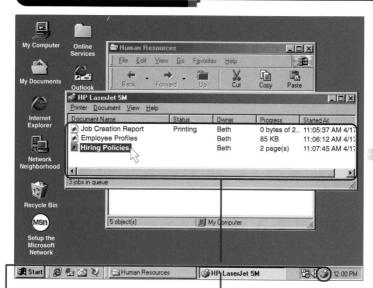

■ When you print a file, the printer icon (🖨) appears in this area.

1 Move the mouse ⌖ over the printer icon (🖨) and then quickly press the left button twice.

■ A window appears, displaying information about the files waiting to print.

2 Move the mouse ⌖ over the file you no longer want to print and then press the left button.

You can stop a file from printing. This is useful if you want to make last-minute changes to the file.

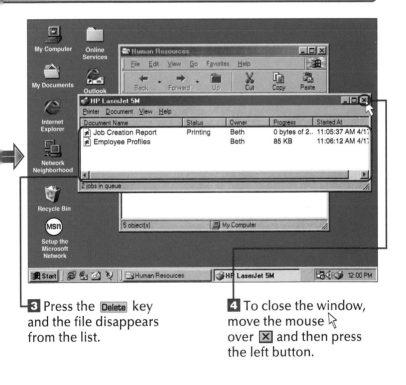

3 Press the Delete key and the file disappears from the list.

4 To close the window, move the mouse ↖ over ✕ and then press the left button.

117

FIND A FILE

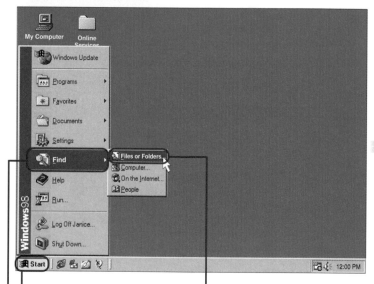

1 Move the mouse ⬡ over **Start** and then press the left button.

2 Move the mouse ⬡ over **Find**.

3 Move the mouse ⬡ over **Files or Folders** and then press the left button.

■ The Find window appears.

118

If you cannot remember the exact name or location of a file you want to work with, you can have Windows search for the file.

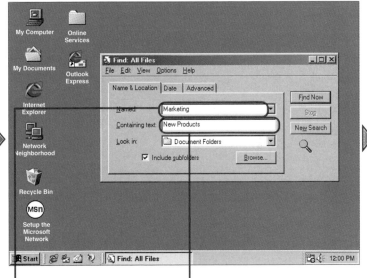

4 To specify the name of the file you want to find, move the mouse I over this area and then press the left button. Then type all or part of the name.

5 To specify a word or phrase within the file you want to find, move the mouse I over this area and then press the left button. Then type the word or phrase.

CONTINUED

119

FIND A FILE

FIND A FILE (CONTINUED)

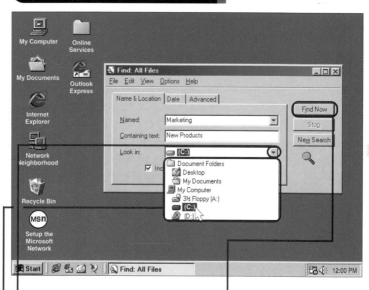

6 To specify where you want Windows to search for the file, move the mouse ⌖ over ▾ in this area and then press the left button.

7 Move the mouse ⌖ over the location you want to search and then press the left button.

8 To start the search, move the mouse ⌖ over **Find Now** and then press the left button.

When the search is complete, Windows displays a list of the files it found. You can open any of these files.

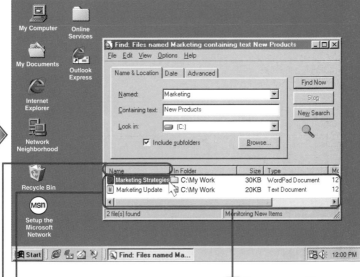

■ This area displays the names of the files Windows found and information about each file.

■ If Windows found several files, move the mouse ⌖ over the **Name** heading and then press the left button to sort the files alphabetically.

9 To open a file, move the mouse ⌖ over the name of the file and then quickly press the left button twice.

121

ADD A SHORTCUT TO THE DESKTOP

ADD A SHORTCUT TO THE DESKTOP

1 Move the mouse ⌖ over the file you want to create a shortcut to and then press the left button.

You can add a
shortcut to the desktop
to provide a quick way of
opening a file you use
regularly.

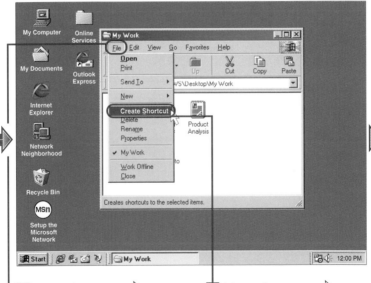

2 Move the mouse ⌖ over **File** and then press the left button.

3 Move the mouse ⌖ over **Create Shortcut** and then press the left button.

CONTINUED

ADD A SHORTCUT TO THE DESKTOP

ADD A SHORTCUT (CONTINUED)

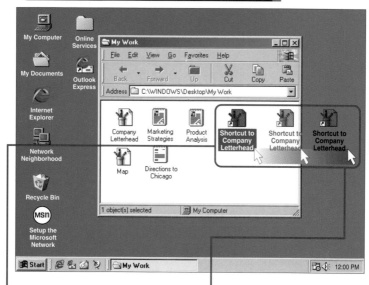

■ Windows creates a shortcut to the file.

4 Position the mouse over the shortcut.

5 Press and hold down the left button as you drag the shortcut to an empty area on your desktop.

124

You can tell the difference between the original file and the shortcut because the shortcut displays an arrow ⤴.

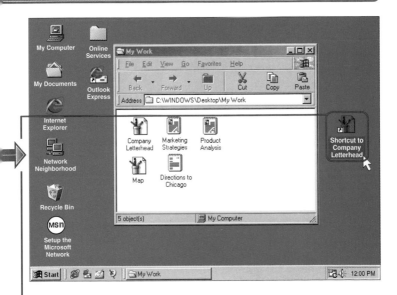

■ The shortcut appears on the desktop.

■ To open the file, move the mouse ⟋ over the shortcut and then quickly press the left button twice.

Note: You can delete a shortcut the same way you delete a file. Deleting a shortcut does not affect the original file. To delete files, see page 108.

125

CHANGE THE DATE AND TIME

CHANGE THE DATE AND TIME

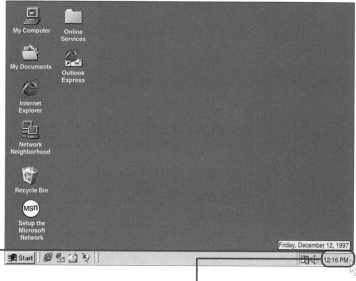

■ This area displays the time set in your computer.

1 To display the date set in your computer, position the mouse ⃟ over this area. A box appears displaying the date.

2 To change the date or time set in your computer, move the mouse ⃟ over this area and then quickly press the left button twice.

You should make
sure the correct date and
time is set in your computer.
Windows uses this information
to determine when you create
and update your
documents.

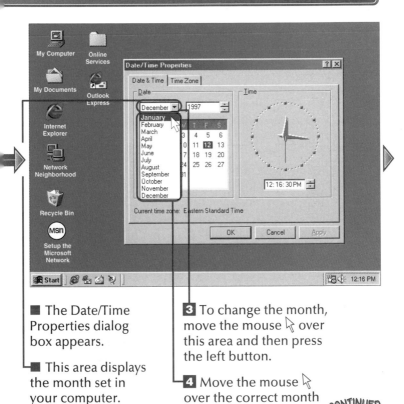

■ The Date/Time
Properties dialog
box appears.

■ This area displays
the month set in
your computer.

3 To change the month,
move the mouse ⍓ over
this area and then press
the left button.

4 Move the mouse ⍓
over the correct month
and then press the left
button.

CONTINUED

127

CHANGE THE DATE AND TIME

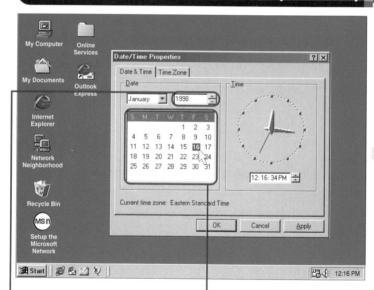

■ This area displays the year set in your computer.

5 To change the year, move the mouse ↖ over ▲ or ▼ and then press the left button.

■ This area displays the days of the month. The current day is highlighted.

6 To change the day, move the mouse ↖ over the correct day and then press the left button.

Your computer has a built-in clock that keeps track of the date and time even when you turn off the computer.

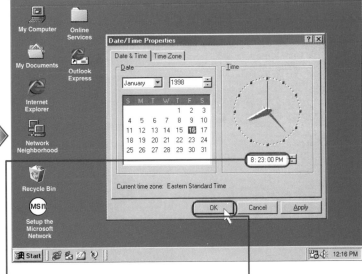

This area displays the time set in your computer.

7 To change the time, move the mouse I over the part of the time you want to change and then quickly press the left button twice. Then type the correct information.

8 To confirm your changes, move the mouse ⟍ over **OK** and then press the left button.

129

ADD WALLPAPER

ADD WALLPAPER

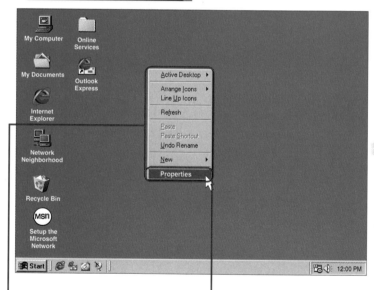

1 Move the mouse ⊠ over a blank area on your desktop and then press the **right** button. A menu appears.

2 Move the mouse ⊠ over **Properties** and then press the left button.

■ The Display Properties dialog box appears.

130

You can decorate your screen by adding wallpaper.

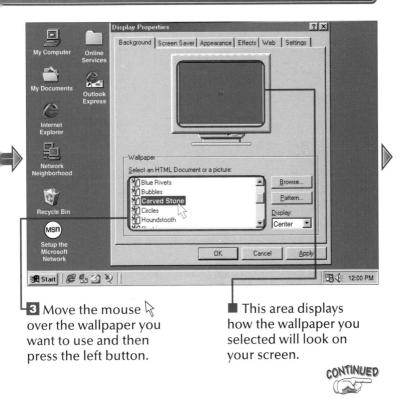

3 Move the mouse ⃗ over the wallpaper you want to use and then press the left button.

■ This area displays how the wallpaper you selected will look on your screen.

CONTINUED

131

ADD WALLPAPER

There are three ways you can display wallpaper on your screen.

Center

Places the wallpaper in the middle of your screen.

ADD WALLPAPER (CONTINUED)

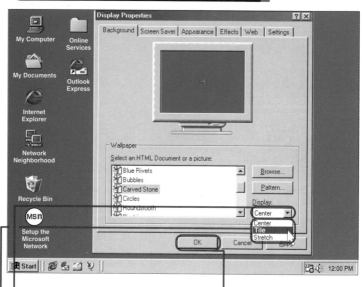

4 To select how you want to display the wallpaper, move the mouse ☐ over this area and then press the left button.

5 Move the mouse ☐ over an option and then press the left button.

6 To add the wallpaper to your screen, move the mouse ☐ over **OK** and then press the left button.

Tile

Repeats the
wallpaper until it
fills your screen.

Stretch

Stretches the
wallpaper to fill
your screen.

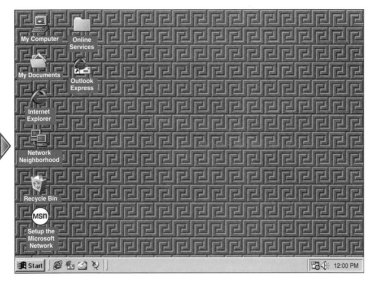

■ The wallpaper appears
on your screen.

■ To remove wallpaper
from your screen, repeat
steps **1** to **3**, selecting
(**None**) in step **3**. Then
perform step **6**.

133

SET UP A SCREEN SAVER

SET UP A SCREEN SAVER

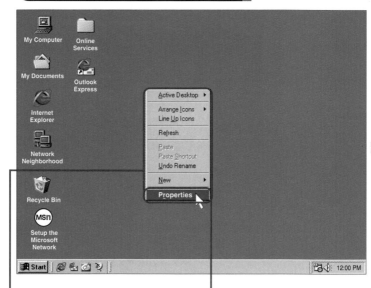

1 Move the mouse ⌕ over a blank area on your desktop and then press the **right** button. A menu appears.

2 Move the mouse ⌕ over **Properties** and then press the left button.

■ The Display Properties dialog box appears.

134

A screen saver is a moving picture or pattern that appears on the screen when you do not use your computer for a period of time.

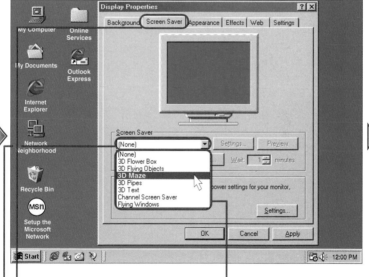

3 Move the mouse ⬚ over the **Screen Saver** tab and then press the left button.

4 To display a list of the available screen savers, move the mouse ⬚ over this area and then press the left button.

5 Move the mouse ⬚ over the screen saver you want to use and then press the left button.

CONTINUED

135

SET UP A SCREEN SAVER

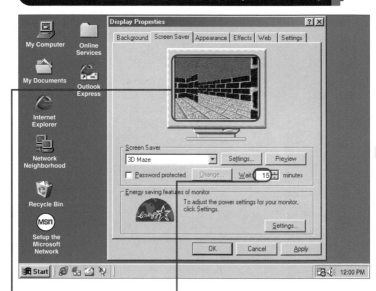

This area displays how the screen saver will look on your screen.

The screen saver will appear when you do not use your computer for the number of minutes shown in this area.

6 To change the number of minutes, move the mouse I over this area and then quickly press the left button twice. Then type a new number.

Screen savers were originally designed to prevent screen burn, which occurs when an image appears in a fixed position on the screen for a period of time.

Today's monitors are better designed to prevent screen burn, but people still use screen savers for their entertainment value.

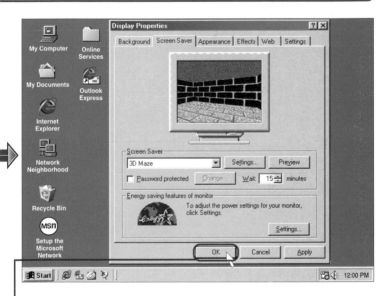

7 To turn on the screen saver, move the mouse over **OK** and then press the left button.

■ When the screen saver appears on your screen, you can move the mouse or press a key on your keyboard to remove the screen saver.

■ To turn off the screen saver, repeat steps 1 to 5, selecting **(None)** in step 5. Then perform step 7.

137

PLAY A MUSIC CD

PLAY A MUSIC CD

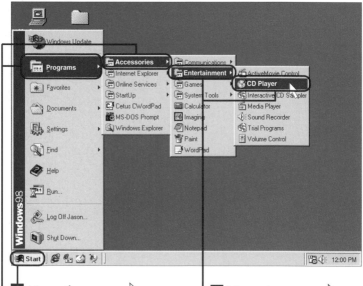

1 Move the mouse 🖑 over **Start** and then press the left button.

2 Move the mouse 🖑 over **Programs**.

3 Move the mouse 🖑 over **Accessories**.

4 Move the mouse 🖑 over **Entertainment**.

5 Move the mouse 🖑 over **CD Player** and then press the left button.

■ The CD Player window appears.

You can use your computer to play music CDs while you work.

You need a CD-ROM drive, a sound card and speakers to play music CDs.

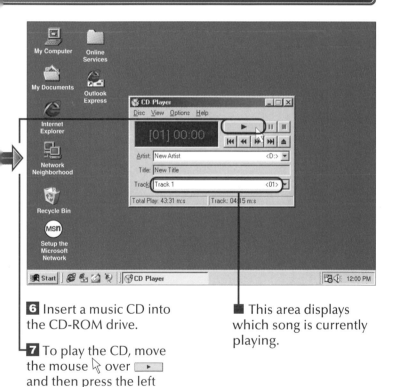

6 Insert a music CD into the CD-ROM drive.

7 To play the CD, move the mouse ⤵ over ▶ and then press the left button.

■ This area displays which song is currently playing.

CONTINUED

139

PLAY A MUSIC CD (CONTINUED)

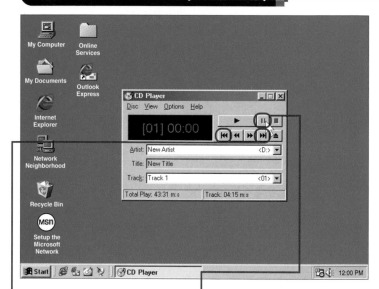

PLAY ANOTHER SONG

1 To play another song on the CD, move the mouse ⌖ over one of these options and then press the left button.

⏮ Play the previous song.

⏭ Play the next song.

PAUSE PLAY

1 To pause the play of the CD, move the mouse ⌖ over ⏸ and then press the left button.

■ To resume the play of the CD, move the mouse ⌖ over ⏸ and then press the left button.

140

You can listen to music privately by plugging a headset into your CD-ROM drive.

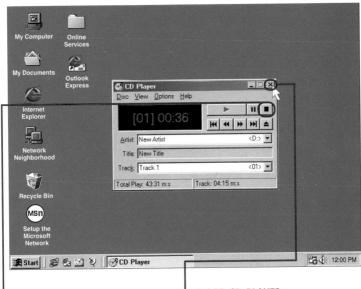

STOP PLAY

1 To stop the play of the CD, move the mouse ↖ over ■ and then press the left button.

CLOSE CD PLAYER

1 When you finish listening to a CD, move the mouse ↖ over ✕ and then press the left button.

ADJUST THE VOLUME

ADJUST THE VOLUME

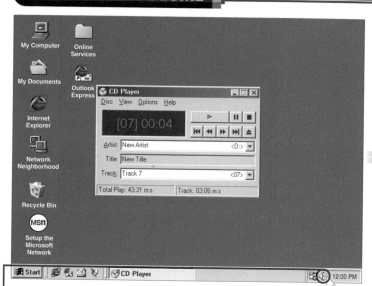

1 To display the Volume control, move the mouse ↖ over ◀€ and then press the left button.

You can easily adjust the volume of sound coming from your speakers.

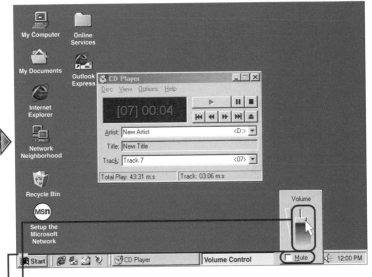

2 Press and hold down the left button as you drag the slider (▭) up or down to increase or decrease the volume.

3 Click this option to turn off the volume (☐ changes to ☑). The speaker icon 🔊 changes to 🔇 on the taskbar.

Note: You can repeat step 3 to once again turn on the volume.

4 To hide the Volume control, move the mouse ⃗ over a blank area on the desktop and then press the left button.

143

CHANGE SCREEN COLORS

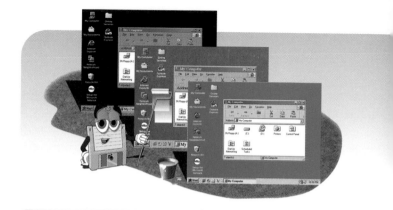

CHANGE SCREEN COLORS

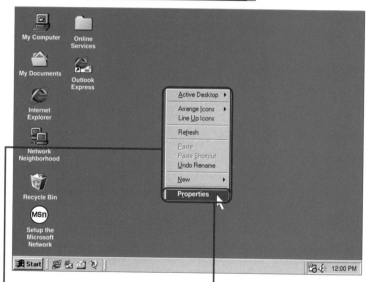

1 Move the mouse ⌖ over a blank area on your desktop and then press the **right** button. A menu appears.

2 Move the mouse ⌖ over **Properties** and then press the left button.

■ The Display Properties dialog box appears.

You can change
the colors displayed on
your screen to personalize
and enhance Windows.

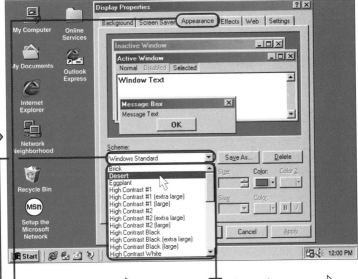

3 Move the mouse ⌖ over
the **Appearance** tab and then
press the left button.

4 To display a list of the
available color schemes,
move the mouse ⌖ over
this area and then press
the left button.

5 Move the mouse ⌖
over the color scheme
you want to use and then
press the left button.

CONTINUED

145

CHANGE SCREEN COLORS

CHANGE SCREEN COLORS (CONTINUED)

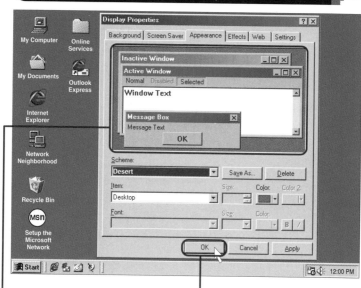

■ This area displays how your screen will look with the color scheme you selected.

6 To add the color scheme, move the mouse ⌂ over **OK** and then press the left button.

Changing the screen colors can make your screen easier to view.

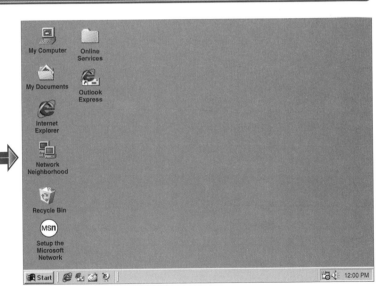

■ Your screen displays the color scheme you selected.

■ To return to the original color scheme, perform steps **1** to **6**, selecting **Windows Standard** in step **5**.

CHANGE SCREEN RESOLUTION

You can change the amount of information that can fit on your screen.

Lower resolutions display larger images on the screen. This lets you see information more clearly.

CHANGE SCREEN RESOLUTION

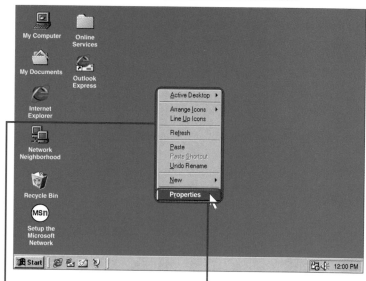

1 Move the mouse ⬚ over a blank area on your desktop and then press the **right** button. A menu appears.

2 Move the mouse ⬚ over **Properties** and then press the left button.

■ The Display Properties dialog box appears.

Higher resolutions display smaller images on the screen. This lets you display more information at once.

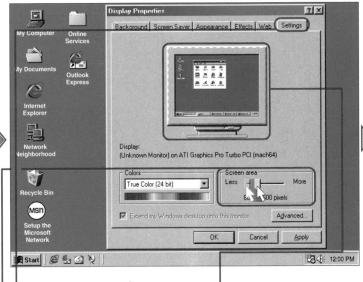

3 Move the mouse ⌖ over the **Settings** tab and then press the left button.

4 To change the resolution, press and hold down the left button as you drag the slider (▯) to select the resolution you want to use.

■ This area displays how your screen will look at the new resolution.

CONTINUED

149

CHANGE SCREEN RESOLUTION

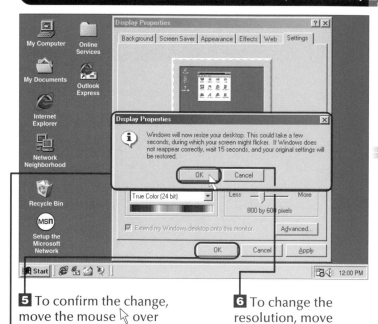

5 To confirm the change, move the mouse ▷ over **OK** and then press the left button.

■ A dialog box appears.

6 To change the resolution, move the mouse ▷ over **OK** and then press the left button.

> Your monitor and video card determine if you can change your screen resolution.

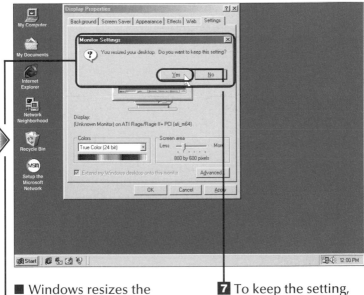

■ Windows resizes the information on your screen.

■ The Monitor Settings dialog box appears, asking if you want to keep the setting.

7 To keep the setting, move the mouse ⟍ over **Yes** and then press the left button.

CHANGE THE WAY YOUR COMPUTER BEHAVES

You can change the way items on your screen look and act. You can choose the Web style or the Classic style.

CHOOSE THE WEB OR CLASSIC STYLE

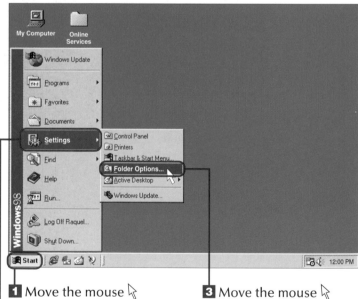

1 Move the mouse ⤢ over **Start** and then press the left button.

2 Move the mouse ⤢ over **Settings**.

3 Move the mouse ⤢ over **Folder Options** and then press the left button.

■ The Folder Options dialog box appears.

Web style

In the Web style, the items on your screen look and act like items on a Web page.

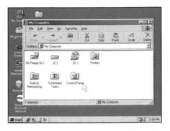

Classic style

In the Classic style, the items on your screen look and act the same way they did in previous versions of Windows.

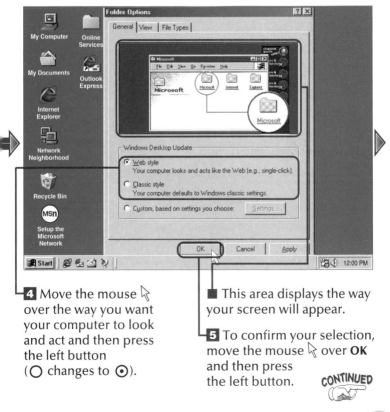

4 Move the mouse ⬚ over the way you want your computer to look and act and then press the left button (○ changes to ⊙).

■ This area displays the way your screen will appear.

5 To confirm your selection, move the mouse ⬚ over **OK** and then press the left button.

CONTINUED

153

CHANGE THE WAY YOUR COMPUTER BEHAVES

The first time you select the Web style, Windows asks if you want to use a single-click rather than a double-click to open items.

WEB OR CLASSIC STYLE (CONTINUED)

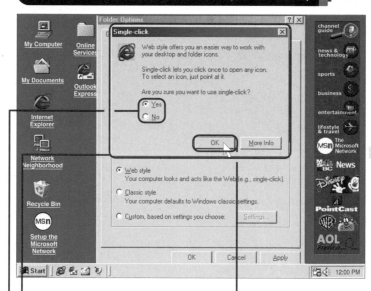

■ A dialog box appears the first time you select the Web style.

6 To specify if you want to open items using a single-click, move the mouse ☒ over an option and then press the left button (○ changes to ⊙).

7 To confirm your selection, move the mouse ☒ over **OK** and then press the left button.

Single-click
Click the left mouse button once.

Double-click
Click the left mouse button twice.

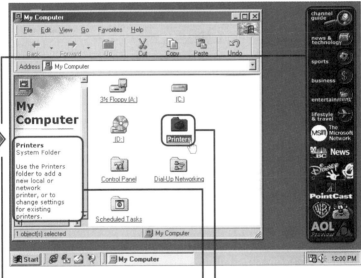

■ When you select the Web style, your computer looks and acts like a Web page.

■ The Channel Bar may appear on your screen. For information on the Channel Bar, see page 222.

■ You can move the mouse 🖑 over an item to select the item.

■ This area displays a description of the selected item.

CHANGE THE WAY YOUR COMPUTER BEHAVES

You can mix and match your favorite settings to customize the way items on your screen look and act.

CHOOSE A CUSTOM STYLE

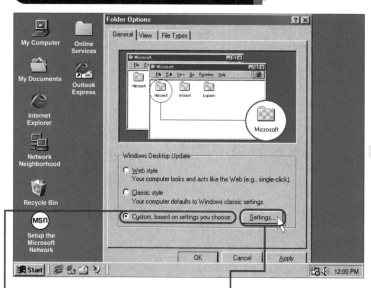

1 To display the Folder Options dialog box, perform steps **1** to **3** on page 152.

2 Move the mouse ⓚ over **Custom** and then press the left button (○ changes to ⊙).

3 To choose your own settings, move the mouse ⓚ over **Settings** and then press the left button.

■ The Custom Settings dialog box appears.

156

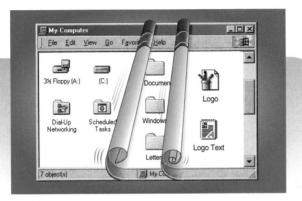

You can choose to open each folder in
the same window or in its own window.

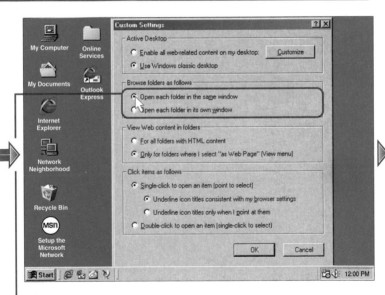

4 To open each folder in
the same window or in its
own window, move the
mouse ⌖ over an option
and then press the left
button (○ changes to ⊙).

CONTINUED

157

CHANGE THE WAY YOUR COMPUTER BEHAVES

Windows offers several settings to customize the way your computer behaves.

CHOOSE A CUSTOM STYLE (CONTINUED)

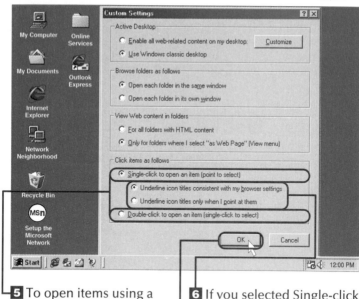

5 To open items using a single-click or a double-click, move the mouse ⬉ over an option and then press the left button (○ changes to ⊙).

6 If you selected Single-click in step **5**, move the mouse ⬉ over an underline option and then press the left button (○ changes to ⊙).

7 Move the mouse ⬉ over **OK** and then press the left button.

You can choose to open items using a single-click or a double-click.

Single-click
Click the left mouse button once.

Double-click
Click the left mouse button twice.

If you choose to open items using a single-click, you can also choose to always underline icon titles or underline icon titles only when you move the mouse over the title.

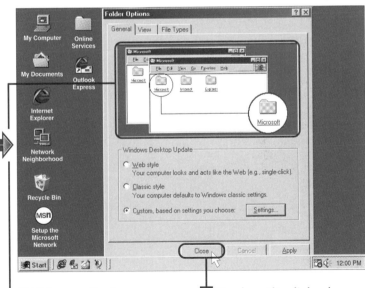

■ This area displays the way your screen will appear.

8 To close the dialog box, move the mouse over **Close** and then press the left button.

159

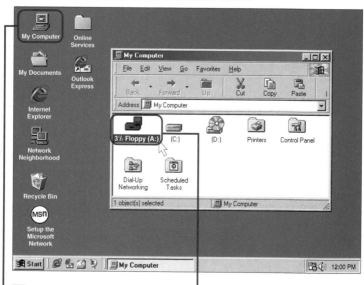

1 Insert the floppy disk you want to format into a drive.

2 Move the mouse ⤢ over **My Computer** and then quickly press the left button twice.

■ The My Computer window appears.

3 Move the mouse ⤢ over the drive containing the floppy disk you want to format (example: A:) and then press the left button.

You must format a floppy disk before you can use the disk to store information.

Floppy disks you buy at computer stores are usually formatted. You may want to later format a disk again to erase the information it contains and prepare the disk for storing new information.

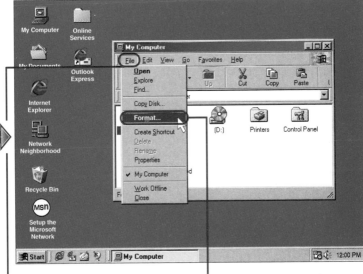

4 Move the mouse over **File** and then press the left button.

5 Move the mouse over **Format** and then press the left button.

■ The Format dialog box appears.

CONTINUED

161

FORMAT A FLOPPY DISK

When formatting a floppy disk, you must tell Windows how much information the disk can store.

FORMAT A FLOPPY DISK (CONTINUED)

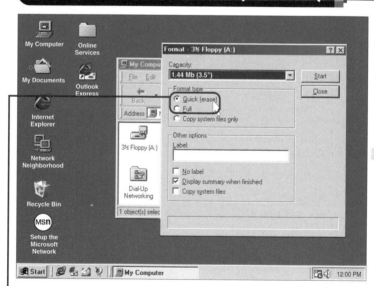

6 Move the mouse ⍺ over the type of format you want to perform and then press the left button (○ changes to ⊙).

Note: If the floppy disk has never been formatted, select the Full option.

Quick (erase)
Removes all files but does not scan the disk for damaged areas.

Full
Removes all files and scans the disk for damaged areas.

Double-Density 720 KB

A 3.5-inch floppy disk that has one hole can store 720 KB of information.

High-Density 1.44 MB

A 3.5-inch floppy disk that has two holes and displays the HD symbol can store 1.44 MB of information.

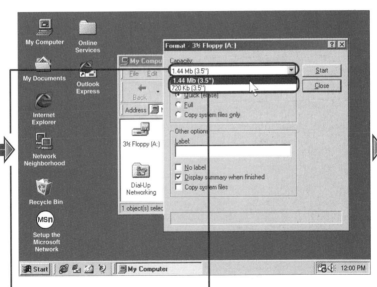

-7 To specify how much information the floppy disk can store, move the mouse ⊹ over this area and then press the left button.

8 Move the mouse ⊹ over the storage capacity of the floppy disk and then press the left button.

CONTINUED

163

FORMAT A FLOPPY DISK

FORMAT A FLOPPY DISK (CONTINUED)

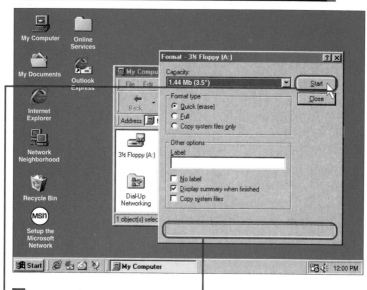

9 To start formatting the floppy disk, move the mouse ⍅ over **Start** and then press the left button.

■ This area will display the progress of the format.

164

Before formatting a floppy disk, make sure the disk does not contain information you may need. Formatting a floppy disk will permanently remove all the information on the disk.

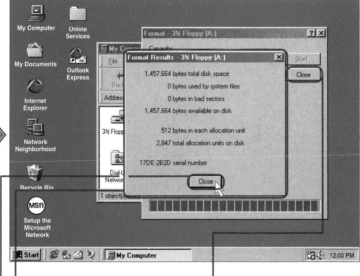

■ The Format Results dialog box appears when the format is complete.

10 To close the dialog box, move the mouse ⟍ over **Close** and then press the left button.

11 To close the Format dialog box, move the mouse ⟍ over **Close** and then press the left button.

DETECT AND REPAIR DISK ERRORS

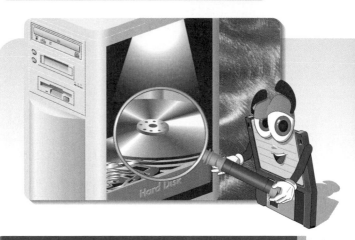

DETECT AND REPAIR DISK ERRORS

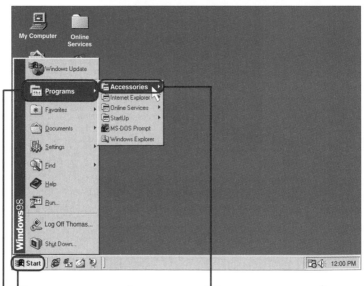

1 Move the mouse over **Start** and then press the left button.

2 Move the mouse over **Programs**.

3 Move the mouse over **Accessories**.

166

You can improve the performance of your computer by using ScanDisk to detect and repair hard disk errors.

The hard disk is the primary device a computer uses to store information.

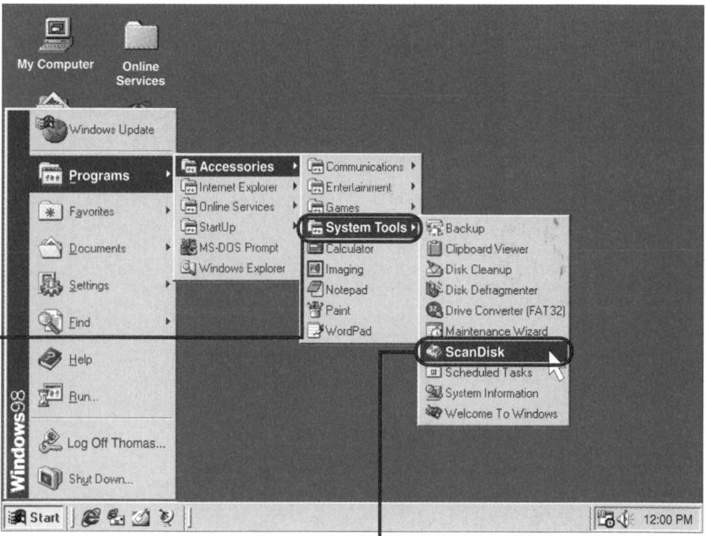

4 Move the mouse over **System Tools**.

5 Move the mouse over **ScanDisk** and then press the left button.

■ The ScanDisk window appears.

CONTINUED

DETECT AND REPAIR DISK ERRORS

DETECT AND REPAIR (CONTINUED)

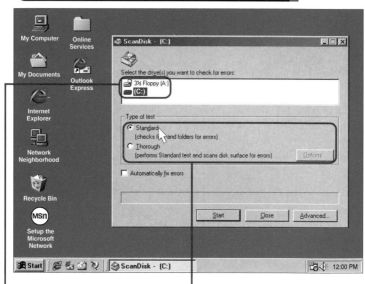

6 Move the mouse ⌖ over the disk you want to check for errors (example: C:) and then press the left button.

7 Move the mouse ⌖ over the type of test you want to perform and then press the left button (○ changes to ⊙).

You must specify what type of test you want ScanDisk to perform.

Standard
Checks files and folders for errors.

Thorough
Checks files, folders and the disk surface for errors.

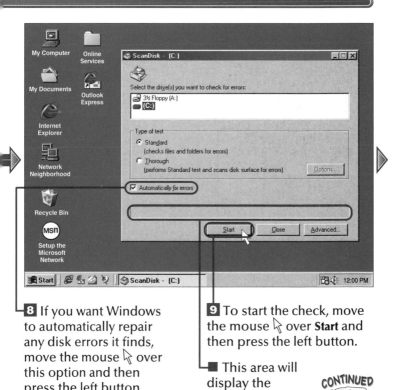

8 If you want Windows to automatically repair any disk errors it finds, move the mouse ⤢ over this option and then press the left button (☐ changes to ☑).

9 To start the check, move the mouse ⤢ over **Start** and then press the left button.

■ This area will display the progress of the check.

CONTINUED

169

DETECT AND REPAIR DISK ERRORS

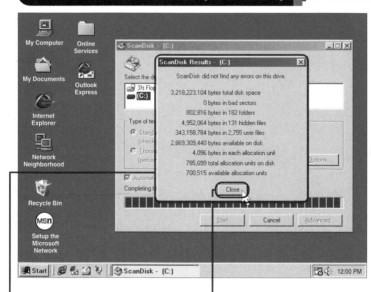

ScanDisk Results - (C:)

ScanDisk did not find any errors on this drive.

3,218,223,104 bytes total disk space
0 bytes in bad sectors
802,816 bytes in 182 folders
4,952,064 bytes in 131 hidden files
343,158,784 bytes in 2,755 user files
2,869,309,440 bytes available on disk
4,096 bytes in each allocation unit
785,699 total allocation units on disk
700,515 available allocation units

■ The ScanDisk Results dialog box appears when the check is complete. The dialog box displays information about the disk.

10 When you finish viewing the information, move the mouse ▷ over **Close** and then press the left button.

You should check your hard disk for errors at least once a month.

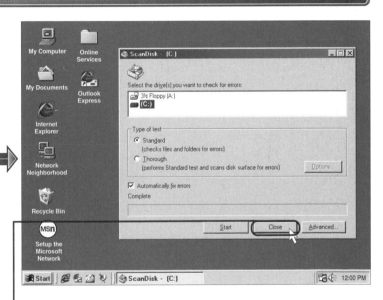

11 To close the ScanDisk window, move the mouse over **Close** and then press the left button.

171

DEFRAGMENT YOUR HARD DISK

DEFRAGMENT YOUR HARD DISK

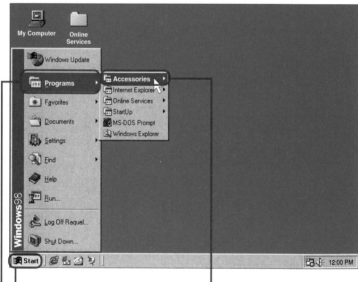

1 Move the mouse ⌖ over **Start** and then press the left button.

2 Move the mouse ⌖ over **Programs**.

3 Move the mouse ⌖ over **Accessories**.

You can improve the performance of your computer by defragmenting your hard disk.

A fragmented hard disk stores parts of a file in many different locations. Your computer must search many areas on the disk to retrieve a file.

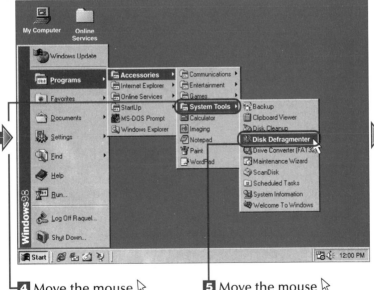

4 Move the mouse ⬚ over **System Tools**.

5 Move the mouse ⬚ over **Disk Defragmenter** and then press the left button.

■ The Select Drive dialog box appears.

CONTINUED

DEFRAGMENT YOUR HARD DISK

DEFRAGMENT HARD DISK (CONTINUED)

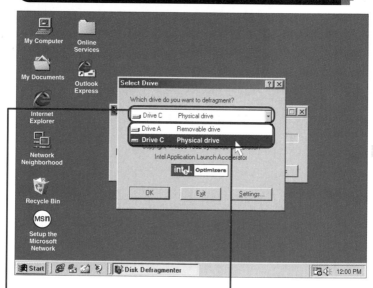

6 To display a list of the drives you can defragment, move the mouse ⮾ over this area and then press the left button.

7 Move the mouse ⮾ over the drive you want to defragment and then press the left button.

You can use Disk Defragmenter to place all the parts of a file in one location. This reduces the time your computer will spend locating the file.

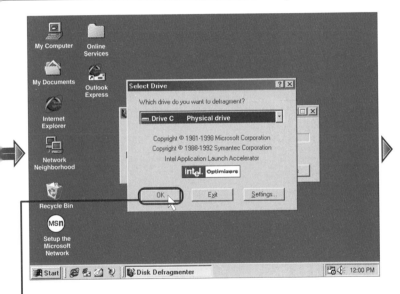

8 To start the defragmentation, move the mouse ⊿ over **OK** and then press the left button.

CONTINUED

DEFRAGMENT YOUR HARD DISK

DEFRAGMENT HARD DISK (CONTINUED)

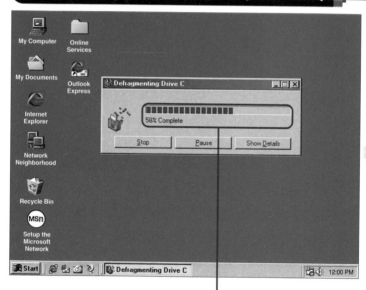

■ The Defragmenting Drive window appears.

■ This area displays the progress of the defragmentation.

You can perform other tasks on your computer while Windows defragments your hard disk, but your computer will operate slower and the defragmentation will take longer.

You should defragment your hard disk at least once a month.

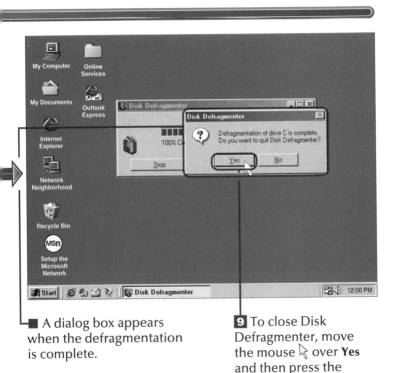

■ A dialog box appears when the defragmentation is complete.

9 To close Disk Defragmenter, move the mouse ↖ over **Yes** and then press the left button.

USING DISK CLEANUP

USING DISK CLEANUP

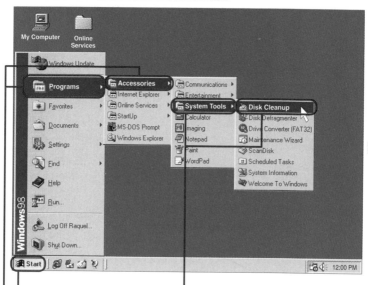

1 Move the mouse ↖ over **Start** and then press the left button.

2 Move the mouse ↖ over **Programs**.

3 Move the mouse ↖ over **Accessories**.

4 Move the mouse ↖ over **System Tools**.

5 Move the mouse ↖ over **Disk Cleanup** and then press the left button.

■ The Select Drive dialog box appears.

Disk Cleanup will remove unnecessary files from your computer to free up disk space.

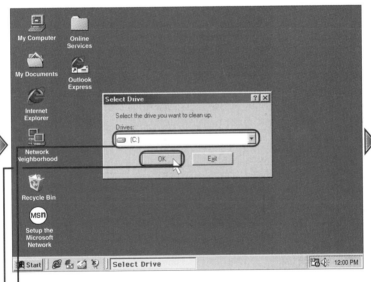

■ This area displays the drive you want to clean up. You can click this area to select a different drive.

6 To continue, move the mouse ⬉ over **OK** and then press the left button.

■ Windows spends a moment calculating how much space you will be able to free up.

■ The Disk Cleanup dialog box appears.

CONTINUED

USING DISK CLEANUP

Temporary Internet Files
Web pages stored on your computer for quick viewing.

Downloaded Program Files
Information transferred from the Internet when you view certain Web pages.

USING DISK CLEANUP (CONTINUED)

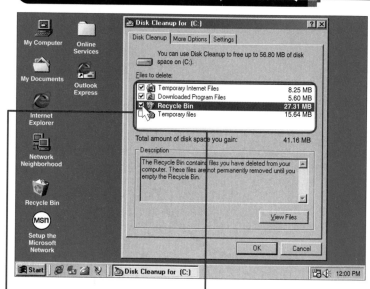

■ This area displays the types of files you can remove and the amount of disk space taken up by each file type.

7 Windows will remove the files for each file type that displays a check mark (✓). To add or remove the check mark, move the mouse ⌖ over the box (☐) beside a file type and then press the left button.

Disk Cleanup can remove several types of files.

Recycle Bin
Files you have deleted.

Temporary Files
Files created by programs for storing temporary information.

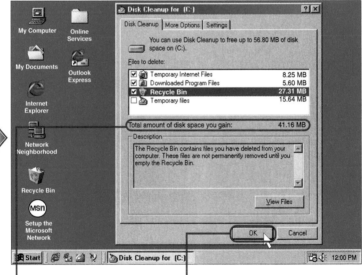

■ This area displays the total space Windows will free up from the file types you selected.

■8 To remove the files, move the mouse ⬚ over **OK** and then press the left button.

■ A confirmation dialog box appears. To close the dialog box, move the mouse ⬚ over **Yes** and then press the left button.

181

START INTERNET EXPLORER

START INTERNET EXPLORER

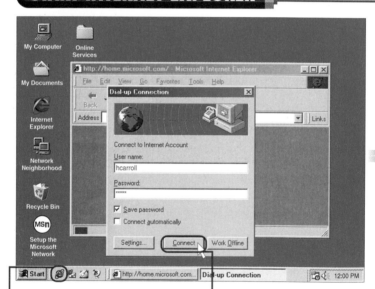

1 To start Internet Explorer, move the mouse ⊾ over 🖝 and then press the left button.

Note: The Internet Connection Wizard appears the first time you start Internet Explorer to help you get connected to the Internet.

■ The Dial-up Connection dialog box appears.

2 To connect to your Internet service provider, move the mouse ⊾ over **Connect** and then press the left button.

You can start Internet Explorer to browse through the information on the Web.

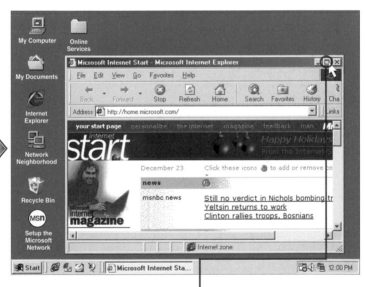

■ The Microsoft Internet Explorer window appears, displaying the Internet Start Web page.

Note: A different Web page may appear on your screen.

3 To maximize the window to fill your screen, move the mouse ⌖ over ▢ and then press the left button.

DISPLAY A SPECIFIC WEB PAGE

DISPLAY A SPECIFIC WEB PAGE

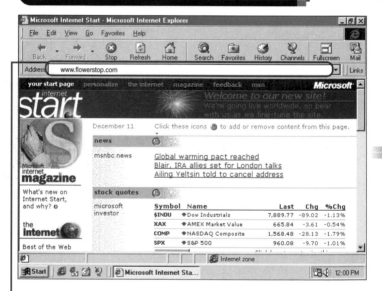

1 To highlight the current Web page address, move the mouse I over this area and then press the left button.

2 Type the address of the Web page you want to view and then press the **Enter** key.

■ When you start typing the address of a Web page you have previously typed, Internet Explorer completes the address for you.

You can easily display a page on the Web that you have heard or read about.

You need to know the address of the Web page you want to view. Each page on the Web has a unique address, called a Uniform Resource Locator (URL).

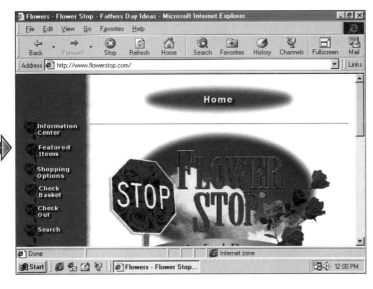

■ The Web page appears on your screen.

SELECT A LINK

SELECT A LINK

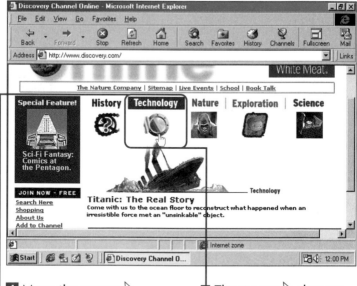

1 Move the mouse ᐅ over a highlighted word or picture of interest and then press the left button.

■ The mouse ᐅ changes to a hand (👆) when over a link.

186

A link connects text or a picture on one Web page to another Web page. When you select the text or picture, the other Web page appears.

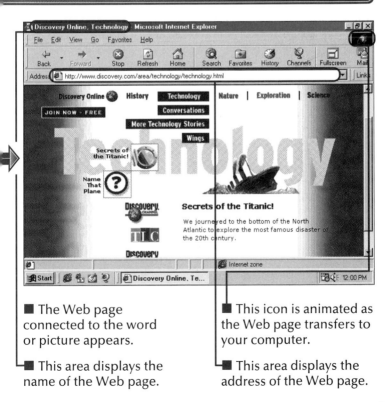

■ The Web page connected to the word or picture appears.

■ This area displays the name of the Web page.

■ This icon is animated as the Web page transfers to your computer.

■ This area displays the address of the Web page.

187

1 To transfer a fresh copy of the displayed Web page to your computer, move the mouse ↕ over **Refresh** and then press the left button.

You can refresh a
Web page to update the
displayed information, such
as the current news. Internet
Explorer will transfer a fresh
copy of the Web page
to your computer.

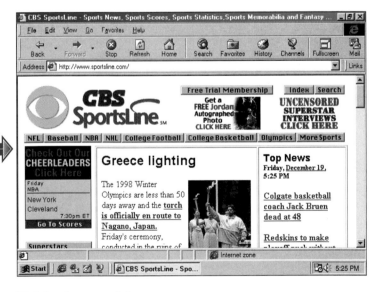

■ A fresh copy of the
Web page appears on
your screen.

STOP TRANSFER
OF INFORMATION

STOP TRANSFER OF INFORMATION

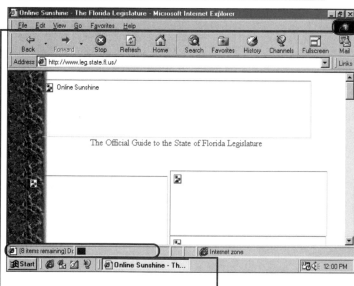

■ The Internet Explorer icon appears animated when information is transferring to your computer.

■ This area shows the progress of the transfer.

If a Web page is taking a long time to appear on your screen, you can stop transferring the page and try connecting again later.

The best time to try connecting to a Web site is during off-peak hours, such as nights and weekends, when fewer people are using the Internet.

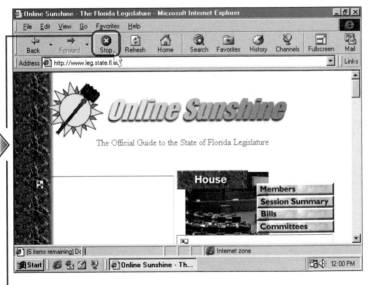

1 To stop the transfer of information, move the mouse ⬡ over **Stop** and then press the left button.

■ You may also want to stop the transfer of information if you realize a Web page is of no interest to you.

191

MOVE THROUGH WEB PAGES

MOVE THROUGH WEB PAGES

1 To display the last Web page you viewed, move the mouse ⅃ over **Back** and then press the left button.

■ To move forward through the Web pages you have viewed, move the mouse ⅃ over **Forward** and then press the left button.

You can easily move back and forth through Web pages you have viewed since you last started Internet Explorer.

You can display a list of the Web pages you have viewed.

1 To display a list of Web pages you have viewed, move the mouse ⌖ over · beside **Back** or **Forward** and then press the left button. A menu appears.

2 Move the mouse ⌖ over the Web page you want to view and then press the left button.

193

DISPLAY YOUR HOME PAGE

DISPLAY YOUR HOME PAGE

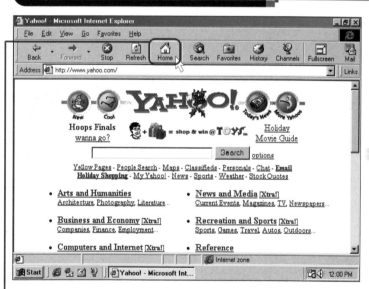

1 To display your home page, move the mouse ⟍ over **Home** and then press the left button.

Your home page is the first page you see when you start Internet Explorer. You can display your home page at any time.

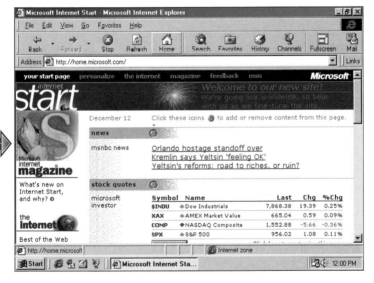

■ Your home page appears.

■ Internet Explorer initially sets the Microsoft Internet Start page as your home page.

Note: Your home page may be different.

195

CHANGE YOUR HOME PAGE

CHANGE YOUR HOME PAGE

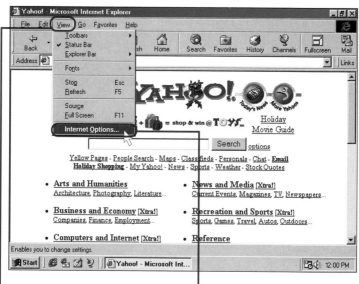

1 Display the Web page you want to set as your home page.

2 Move the mouse ⅄ over **View** and then press the left button.

3 Move the mouse ⅄ over **Internet Options** and then press the left button.

■ The Internet Options dialog box appears.

You can choose any page
on the Web as your home page.
You may want to choose a page
that provides a good starting
point for exploring the Web. Your
home page can also be your
favorite Web page.

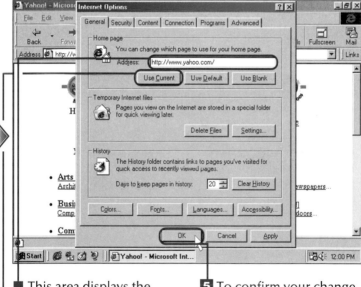

■ This area displays the
address of your current
home page.

4 To set the Web page
displayed on your screen
as your new home page,
move the mouse ⫯ over
Use Current and then
press the left button.

5 To confirm your change,
move the mouse ⫯ over **OK**
and then press the left
button.

197

START OUTLOOK EXPRESS

START OUTLOOK EXPRESS

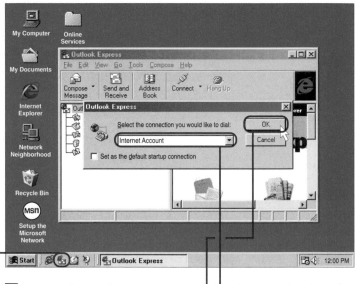

1 To start Outlook Express, move the mouse ⫣ over 🐦 and then press the left button.

Note: The Internet Connection Wizard appears the first time you start Outlook Express to help you get connected to the Internet.

■ This area displays the connection Windows will dial.

2 To connect to your service provider, move the mouse ⫣ over **OK** and then press the left button.

You can start
Outlook Express to
exchange e-mail messages
with people around
the world.

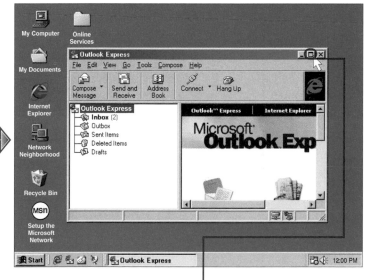

■ The Outlook Express
window appears.

3 To maximize the Outlook
Express window to fill your
screen, move the mouse ⬉
over 🔲 and then press the
left button.

THE MAIL FOLDERS

Outlook Express uses five folders to store your messages.

Inbox
Stores messages sent to you.

Outbox
Temporarily stores messages you have not yet sent.

THE MAIL FOLDERS

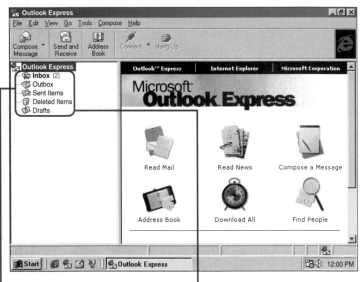

■ This area displays the mail folders that store your messages.

■ The number in brackets beside a folder indicates how many unread messages the folder contains. The number disappears when you have read all the messages in the folder.

Sent Items

Stores copies of messages you have sent.

Deleted Items

Stores messages you have deleted.

Drafts

Stores messages you have not yet completed.

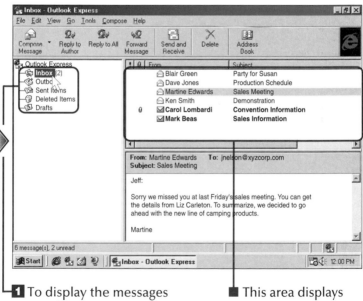

1 To display the messages in a mail folder, move the mouse ⌖ over a folder and then press the left button. The folder is highlighted.

■ This area displays the messages in the highlighted folder.

READ MESSAGES

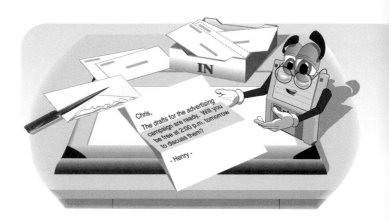

READ MESSAGES

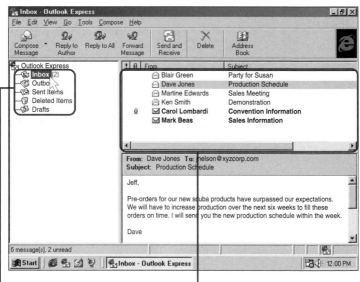

1 Move the mouse ⌖ over the folder containing the messages you want to read and then press the left button. The folder is highlighted.

■ This area displays the messages in the highlighted folder. Messages you have not read display a closed envelope (✉) and appear in **bold** type.

202

You can easily open your messages to read their contents.

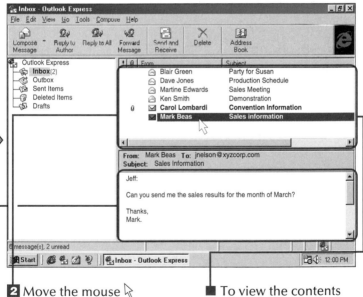

2 Move the mouse ↖ over a message you want to read and then press the left button.

■ The contents of the message appear in this area.

■ To view the contents of another message, move the mouse ↖ over the message and then press the left button.

203

GET NEW MESSAGES

GET NEW MESSAGES

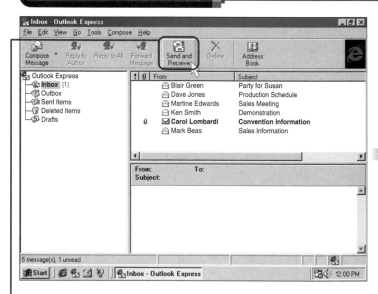

1 To immediately check for new messages, move the mouse ⟋ over **Send and Receive** and then press the left button.

Outlook Express automatically checks for new messages every 30 minutes. You can check for new messages at any time.

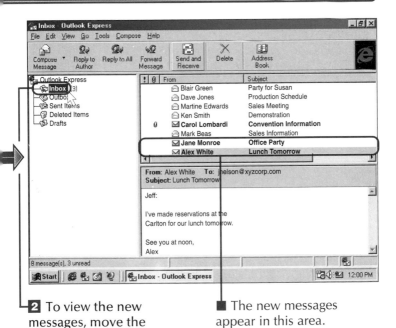

2 To view the new messages, move the mouse ⫣ over the **Inbox** folder and then press the left button.

■ The new messages appear in this area.

205

COMPOSE A MESSAGE

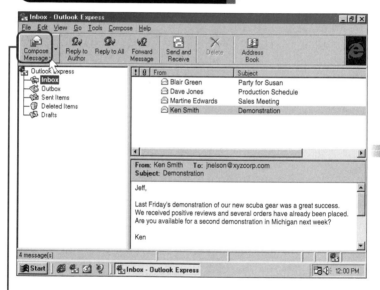

1 Move the mouse ⌕ over **Compose Message** and then press the left button.

■ The New Message window appears.

You can compose and then send a message to exchange ideas or request information.

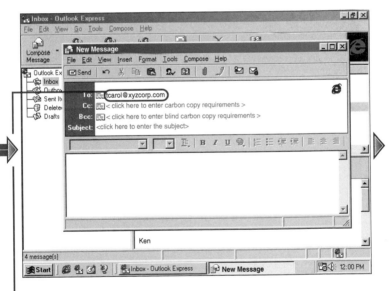

2 Type the e-mail address of the person you want to receive the message.

CONTINUED

207

When composing a message, you can choose to send copies of the message to other people.

COMPOSE A MESSAGE (CONTINUED)

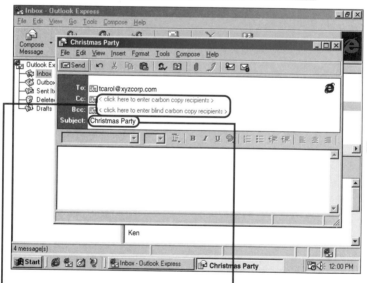

3 To send a copy of the message to another person, move the mouse I over one of these areas and then press the left button. Then type the e-mail address.

4 Move the mouse I over this area and then press the left button. Then type the subject of the message.

Carbon Copy (Cc)

Send an exact copy of the message to a person who is not directly involved, but would be interested in the message.

Blind Carbon Copy (Bcc)

Send an exact copy of the message to a person without anyone else knowing that the person received the message.

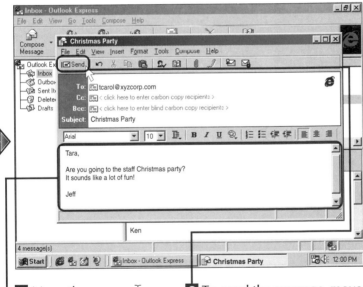

5 Move the mouse I over this area and then press the left button. Then type the message.

6 To send the message, move the mouse ↘ over **Send** and then press the left button.

Note: Outlook Express stores a copy of each message you send in the Sent Items folder.

209

ATTACH A FILE TO A MESSAGE

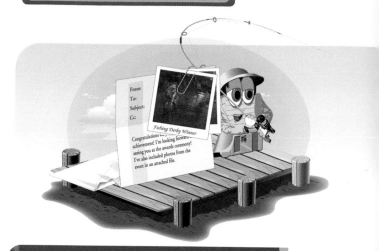

ATTACH A FILE TO A MESSAGE

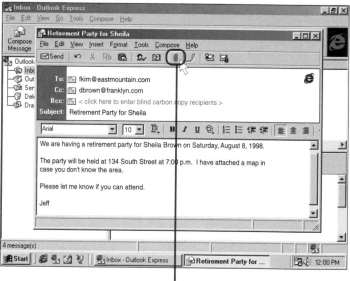

1 To compose a message, perform steps **1** to **5** starting on page 206.

2 To attach a file to the message, move the mouse over 📎 and then press the left button.

■ The Insert Attachment dialog box appears.

You can attach
a file to a message you
are sending. Attaching a file is
useful when you want to include
additional information with
a message.

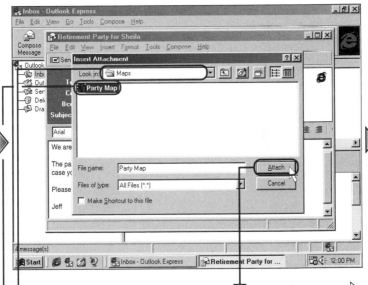

■ This area shows the
location of the displayed files.

■3 Move the mouse ⇱ over
the name of the file you want
to attach to the message and
then press the left button.

4 Move the mouse ⇱
over **Attach** and then
press the left button.

CONTINUED

ATTACH A FILE TO A MESSAGE (CONTINUED)

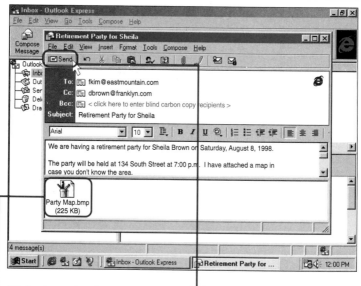

■ An icon for the file you selected appears in the message.

5 To send the message, move the mouse ⤢ over **Send** and then press the left button.

212

You can attach
files such as documents,
pictures, programs, sounds
and videos to a
message.

The computer receiving the
message must have the necessary
hardware and software to display
or play the file.

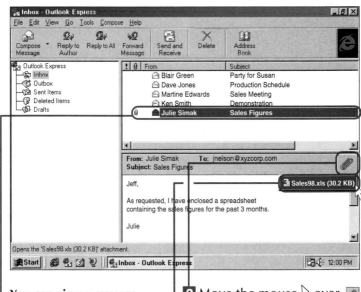

**You can view a message
with an attached file.**

1 Move the mouse ⌕
over a message with an
attached file and then
press the left button.

2 Move the mouse ⌕ over ✎
and then press the left button.

3 Move the mouse ⌕ over
the file you want to open and
then press the left button.

■ A dialog box may appear,
asking if you want to open
or save the file.

213

REPLY TO A MESSAGE

REPLY TO A MESSAGE

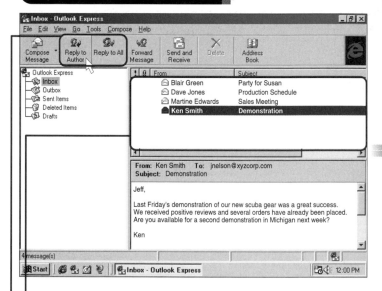

1 Move the mouse ⬉ over the message you want to reply to and then press the left button.

2 Move the mouse ⬉ over the reply option you want to use and then press the left button.

Reply to Author
Send a reply to the author only.

Reply to All
Send a reply to the author and everyone who received the original message.

214

You can reply to a message to answer a question or comment on the message.

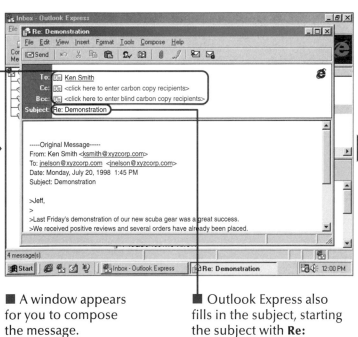

■ A window appears for you to compose the message.

■ Outlook Express fills in the e-mail address(es) for you.

■ Outlook Express also fills in the subject, starting the subject with **Re:**

CONTINUED

REPLY TO
A MESSAGE

REPLY TO A MESSAGE (CONTINUED)

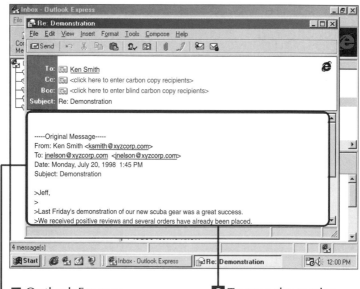

■ Outlook Express includes a copy of the original message to help the reader identify which message you are replying to. This is called quoting.

3 To save the reader time, delete all parts of the original message that do not directly relate to your reply.

When sending and
replying to messages, you
can use special characters to
express emotions. These
characters resemble human
faces if you turn them
sideways.

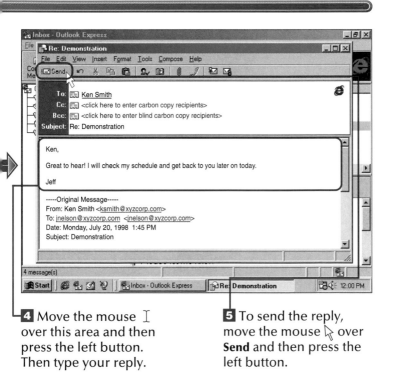

4 Move the mouse I
over this area and then
press the left button.
Then type your reply.

5 To send the reply,
move the mouse ⬄ over
Send and then press the
left button.

217

FORWARD A MESSAGE

FORWARD A MESSAGE

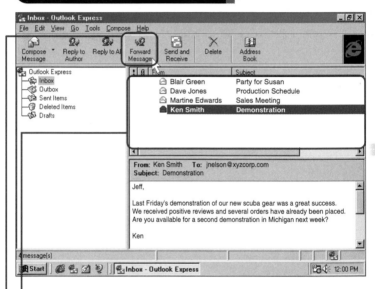

1 Move the mouse ⌖ over the message you want to forward and then press the left button.

2 Move the mouse ⌖ over **Forward Message** and then press the left button.

■ A window appears, displaying the message you are forwarding.

After reading a message, you can add comments and then forward the message to a friend or colleague.

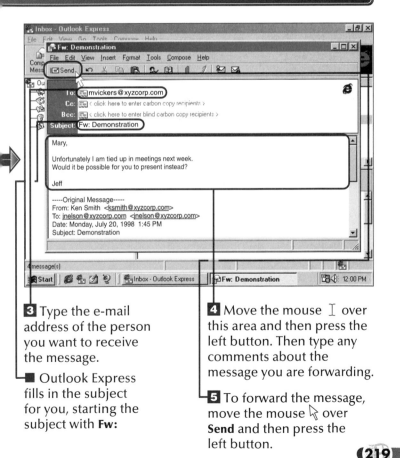

3 Type the e-mail address of the person you want to receive the message.

■ Outlook Express fills in the subject for you, starting the subject with **Fw:**

4 Move the mouse I over this area and then press the left button. Then type any comments about the message you are forwarding.

5 To forward the message, move the mouse ⟋ over **Send** and then press the left button.

DELETE A MESSAGE

DELETE A MESSAGE

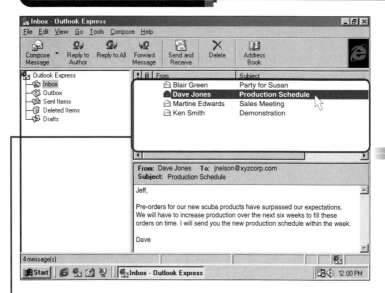

1 Move the mouse ⌖ over the message you want to delete and then press the left button.

2 Press the Delete key.

You can delete
a message you no longer
need. Deleting messages
prevents your folders from
becoming cluttered with
messages.

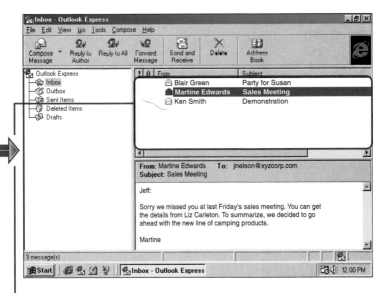

■ Outlook Express
removes the message
from the current folder
and places the message
in the Deleted Items
folder.

Note: Deleting a message
from the Deleted Items folder
will permanently remove the
message from your computer.

221

ADD A CHANNEL

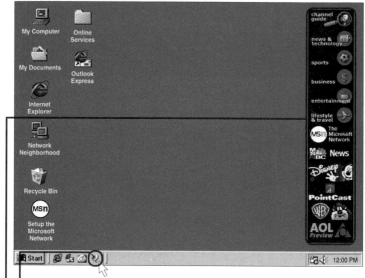

1 To view your channels, move the mouse ⌖ over 🌐 and then press the left button.

■ To quickly view a channel displayed on the Channel Bar, move the mouse ⌖ over the channel and then press the left button.

Note: A dialog box may appear, asking if you want to download the most current content. You should connect to the Internet to continue.

A channel is a Web
site that automatically
delivers information from the
Internet to your computer.
You can add channels
of interest to you.

■2 Move the mouse ▷
to the left side of your
screen to view the
channels you can add
(▷ changes to ⑦).

■3 Move the mouse ⑦ over
a category of interest and
then press the left button.

CONTINUED

ADD A CHANNEL

Channel Screen Saver

Your channel subscription includes content for display by the
Channel Screen Saver. Would you like to replace your current
screen saver with the Channel Screen Saver?

☐ Do not ask me again

Yes

ADD A CHANNEL (CONTINUED)

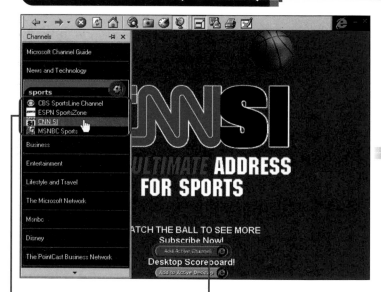

Channels
Microsoft Channel Guide
News and Technology

sports
CBS SportsLine Channel
ESPN SportsZone
CNN SI
MSNBC Sports

Business
Entertainment
Lifestyle and Travel
The Microsoft Network
Msnbc
Disney
The PointCast Business Network

ULTIMATE **ADDRESS**
FOR SPORTS

ATCH THE BALL TO SEE MORE
Subscribe Now!
Add Active Channel
Desktop Scoreboard!
Add to Active Desktop

■ A list of channels in
the category appears.

4 Move the mouse ↸
over a channel of interest
and then press the left
button.

■ The channel appears.

5 Move the mouse ↸
over **Add Active Channel** or
the button that allows you
to add the channel and
then press the left button.

224

When adding a channel, a dialog box may appear that allows you to replace your current screen saver with the channel screen saver.

The screen saver will appear on your screen when you do not use your computer for a period of time.

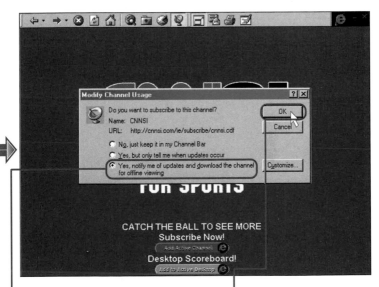

■ A dialog box appears.

6 To be notified of updates and to transfer the channel to your computer, move the mouse ⌖ over this option and then press the left button (○ changes to ⊙).

7 To add the channel, move the mouse ⌖ over **OK** and then press the left button.

225

ADD AN ACTIVE DESKTOP ITEM

ADD AN ACTIVE DESKTOP ITEM

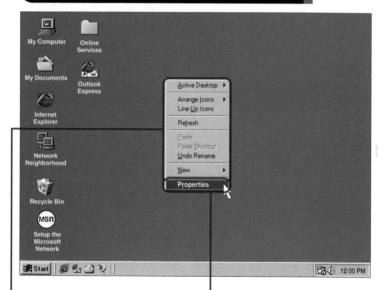

1 Move the mouse ↖ over a blank area on your desktop and then press the **right** button. A menu appears.

2 Move the mouse ↖ over **Properties** and then press the left button.

■ The Display Properties dialog box appears.

You can add active content from the Web to your desktop. Active content is information that changes on your screen, such as a stock ticker or a weather map.

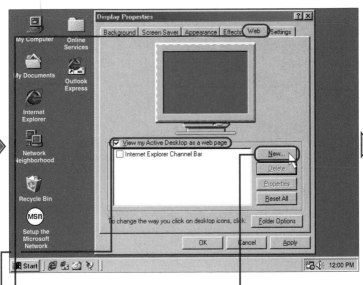

3 Move the mouse ⬚ over the **Web** tab and then press the left button.

4 This option must display a check mark (☑) to add Active Desktop items. To add a check mark, move the mouse ⬚ over this option and then press the left button.

5 To add an Active Desktop item, move the mouse ⬚ over **New** and then press the left button.

CONTINUED

227

ADD AN ACTIVE DESKTOP ITEM

ADD ACTIVE ITEM (CONTINUED)

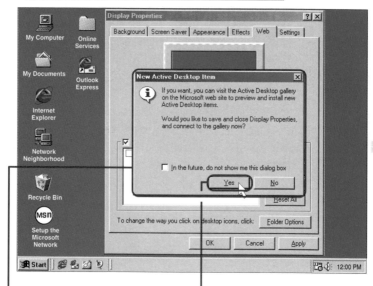

■ A dialog box appears, asking if you want to visit the gallery where you can see a list of Active Desktop items.

6 To visit the gallery, move the mouse ⟍ over **Yes** and then press the left button.

Note: If you are not connected to the Internet, a dialog box may appear that allows you to connect.

The Active Desktop Gallery offers various items you can add to your desktop. The items are organized into categories such as news, sports, entertainment and weather.

■ Internet Explorer opens and the Active Desktop Gallery appears.

*Note: A Security Warning dialog box may appear, asking you to install and run a program. To continue, move the mouse ▷ over **Yes** and then press the left button.*

7 To display Active Desktop items of interest, move the mouse 🖑 over a category and then press the left button.

■ This area displays the Active Desktop items in the category you selected.

CONTINUED

229

ADD AN ACTIVE DESKTOP ITEM

ADD ACTIVE ITEM (CONTINUED)

8 Move the mouse 👆 over an Active Desktop item of interest and then press the left button.

■ Information about the item appears.

Note: You can repeat steps 7 and 8 to view information about other items.

9 To add the displayed item to your desktop, move the mouse 👆 over **Add to Active Desktop** and then press the left button.

When you find an Active Desktop item of interest in the gallery, you can easily add the item to your desktop.

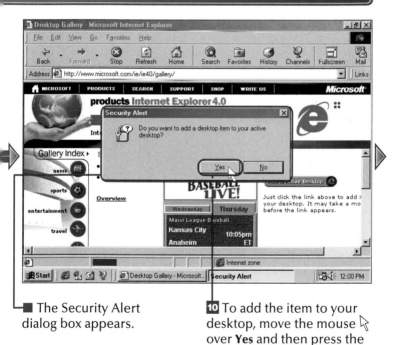

■ The Security Alert dialog box appears.

10 To add the item to your desktop, move the mouse over **Yes** and then press the left button.

CONTINUED

ADD AN ACTIVE DESKTOP ITEM

ADD ACTIVE ITEM (CONTINUED)

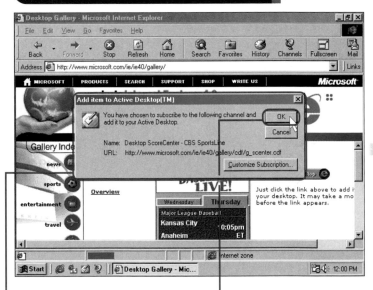

■ Windows indicates that you have chosen to subscribe to the channel and add it to your desktop.

11 To continue, move the mouse ℝ over **OK** and then press the left button.

■ Windows copies the necessary information to your computer.

An Active Desktop item will automatically update to display the most current information on your screen.

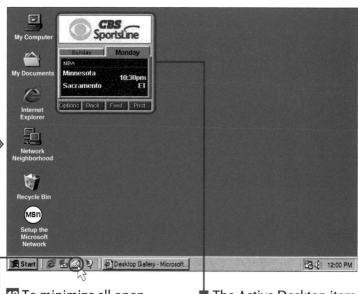

◄ 12 To minimize all open windows so you can clearly view your desktop, move the mouse ⟋ over 🖉 and then press the left button.

■ The Active Desktop item appears on your screen.

Note: To move an item, see page 234. To remove an item, see page 236.

233

MOVE AN ACTIVE DESKTOP ITEM

1 Position the mouse ⌖ over the top edge of the item. A gray bar appears.

2 Press and hold down the left button as you drag the item to a new location on your screen.

You can move an
Active Desktop item
to a new location on
your screen.

■ The item appears in
the new location.

REMOVE OR DISPLAY AN ACTIVE DESKTOP ITEM

REMOVE OR DISPLAY AN ACTIVE DESKTOP ITEM

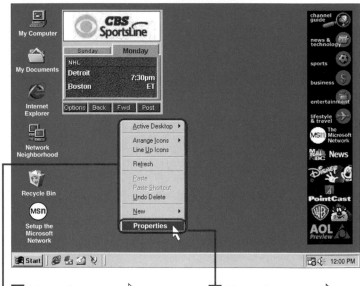

1 Move the mouse 🔍 over a blank area on your desktop and then press the **right** button. A menu appears.

2 Move the mouse 🔍 over **Properties** and then press the left button.

■ The Display Properties dialog box appears.

236

You can temporarily remove an Active Desktop item you no longer want to appear on your desktop. You can redisplay the item at any time.

The Internet Explorer Channel Bar is an Active Desktop item that appears when you first start Windows. You can remove or display the Channel Bar as you would any other Active Desktop item.

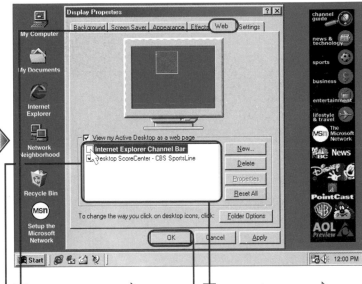

3 Move the mouse ⍾ over the **Web** tab and then press the left button.

■ Each item that displays a check mark (☑) appears on your desktop.

4 Move the mouse ⍾ over the box beside the item you want to remove (☐) or display (☑) and then press the left button.

5 Move the mouse ⍾ over **OK** and then press the left button.

237

INDEX

INDEX

INDEX

OVER 5 MILLION

OTHER 3-D Visual SERIES

SIMPLIFIED SERIES

NOW AVAILABLE!

Windows 98 Simplified

ISBN 0-7645-6030-1
$24.99 USA/£23.99 UK

Windows 95 Simplified

ISBN 1-56884-662-2
$19.99 USA/£18.99 UK

More Windows 95 Simplified

ISBN 1-56884-689-4
$19.99 USA/£18.99 UK

Word 6 For Windows Simplified

ISBN 1-56884-660-6
$19.99 USA/£18.99 UK

Excel 97 Simplified

ISBN 0-7645-6022-0
$24.99 USA/£23.99 UK

Excel For Windows 95 Simplified

ISBN 1-56884-682-7
$19.99 USA/£18.99 UK

Creating Web Pages Simplified

ISBN 0-7645-6007-7
$24.99 USA/£23.99 UK

Internet and World Wide Web Simplified, 2nd Ed.

ISBN 0-7645-6029-8
$24.99 USA/£23.99 UK

Computers Simplified, Third Edition

ISBN 0-7645-6008-5
$24.99 USA/£23.99 UK

FOR CORPORATE ORDERS, PLEASE CALL: 800-469-6616

S A T I S F I E D   U S E R S !

Windows 3.1 Simplified
ISBN 1-56884-654-1
$19.99 USA/£18.99 UK

Word 97 Simplified
ISBN 0-7645-6011-5
$24.99 USA/£23.99 UK

Word For Windows 95 Simplified
ISBN 1-56884-681-9
$19.99 USA/£18.99 UK

Excel 5 For Windows Simplified
ISBN 1-56884-664-9
$19.99 USA/£18.99 UK

Office 97 Simplified
ISBN 0-7645-6009-3
$29.99 USA/£28.99 UK

Microsoft Office 4.2 For Windows Simplified
ISBN 1-56884-673-8
$27.99 USA/£26.99 UK

The 3-D Visual Dictionary of Computing
ISBN 1-56884-678-9
$19.99 USA/£18.99 UK

WordPerfect 6.1 For Windows Simplified
ISBN 1-56884-665-7
$19.99 USA/£18.99 UK

Lotus 1-2-3 R5 For Windows Simplified
ISBN 1-56884-670-3
$19.99 USA/£18.99 UK

FOR CORPORATE ORDERS, PLEASE CALL: 800-469-6616

OVER 5 MILLION

OTHER 3-D Visual SERIES

TEACH YOURSELF VISUALLY SERIES

NOW AVAILABLE!
Teach Yourself Windows 98 VISUALLY
ISBN 0-7645-6025-5
$29.99 USA/£28.99 UK

Also Available!
Teach Yourself Networking VISUALLY
ISBN 0-7645-6023-9
$29.99 USA/£28.99 UK

Teach Yourself Computers and the Internet VISUALLY
ISBN 0-7645-6002-6
$29.99 USA/£28.99 UK

Teach Yourself Windows 95 VISUALLY
ISBN 0-7645-6001-8
$29.99 USA/£28.99 UK

Teach Yourself Office 97 VISUALLY
ISBN 0-7645-6018-2
$29.99 USA/£28.99 UK

Teach Yourself the Internet and World Wide Web VISUALLY
ISBN 0-7645-6020-4
$29.99 USA/£28.99 UK

Teach Yourself Access 97 VISUALLY
ISBN 0-7645-6026-3
$29.99 USA/£28.99 UK

Teach Yourself Netscape Navigator 4 VISUALLY
ISBN 0-7645-6028-X
$29.99 USA/£28.99 UK

Teach Yourself Word 97 VISUALLY
ISBN 0-7645-6032-8
$29.99 USA/£28.99 UK

Visit our Web site at:
http://www.maran.com

FOR CORPORATE ORDERS, PLEASE CALL: 800-469-6616

S A T I S F I E D   U S E R S !

MASTER VISUALLY SERIES

NOW AVAILABLE!
Master Windows 98 VISUALLY
ISBN 0-7645-6034-4
$39.99 USA/£36.99 UK

Master Windows 95 VISUALLY
ISBN 0-7645-6024-7
$39.99 USA/£36.99 UK

POCKETGUIDES

Windows 95 Visual PocketGuide
ISBN 1-56884-661-4
$14.99 USA/£13.99 UK

Word 6 For Windows Visual PocketGuide
ISBN 1-56884-666-5
$14.99 USA/£13.99 UK

ALSO AVAILABLE:

Windows 3.1 Visual PocketGuide
ISBN 1-56884-650-9
$14.99 USA/£13.99 UK

Excel 5 For Windows Visual PocketGuide
ISBN 1-56884-667-3
$14.99 USA/£13.99 UK

WordPerfect 6.1 For Windows Visual PocketGuide
ISBN 1-56884-668-1
$14.99 USA/£13.99 UK

FOR CORPORATE ORDERS, PLEASE CALL: **800-469-6616**

ORDER FORM

IDG BOOKS

TRADE & INDIVIDUAL ORDERS

Phone: **(800) 762-2974**
or **(317) 895-5200**
(8 a.m.–6 p.m., CST, weekdays)
FAX : **(317) 895-5298**

CORPORATE ORDERS FOR 3-D VISUAL™ SERIES

Phone: **(800) 469-6616**
(8 a.m.–5 p.m., EST, weekdays)
FAX : **(905) 890-9434**

EDUCATIONAL ORDERS & DISCOUNTS

Phone: **(800) 434-2086**
(8:30 a.m.–5 p.m., CST, weekdays)
FAX : **(817) 251-8174**

Qty	ISBN	Title	Price	Total

Shipping & Handling Charges

	Description	**First book**	**Each add'l. book**	**Total**
Domestic	Normal	$4.50	$1.50	$
	Two Day Air	$8.50	$2.50	$
	Overnight	$18.00	$3.00	$
International	Surface	$8.00	$8.00	$
	Airmail	$16.00	$16.00	$
	DHL Air	$17.00	$17.00	$

Subtotal _____

CA residents add
applicable sales tax _____

IN, MA and MD
residents add
5% sales tax _____

IL residents add
6.25% sales tax _____

RI residents add
7% sales tax _____

TX residents add
8.25% sales tax _____

Shipping _____

Total _____

Ship to:

Name_____

Address _____

Company_____

City/State/Zip _____

Daytime Phone _____

Payment: □ Check to IDG Books (US Funds Only)
□ Visa   □ Mastercard   □ American Express

Card # _____ Exp. _____

Signature_____

maranGraphics